The
Honest
Truth

Real Happenings
Far Funnier than Fiction

STEVE LEINER
Illustrations by L. PLUME

The Honest Truth: Real Happenings Far Funnier than Fiction
Published by Rebelea Publications
San Francisco, CA

ISBN: 979-8-9902668-0-3
Humor

Cover and Interior Design by Victoria Wolf, wolfdesignandmarketing.com, copyright owned by Steven Leiner.

rebelea
publications

To Rebecca and Leah

Contents

Language's Curiosities: Watch What You're Saying

COVID: Panning the Pandemic

Educational Pearls: My, How We Learn

Technology: Perfection's Challenges

From My Travels: Hello World

Humor: LOL

Medical Miscellany: Meet the Doctor

Introduction

One thing that's kept my spirits up as I make my way through life are the many ironic situations I've come across first- or second-hand or through the news. Some are outright absurdities, others subtler. Regardless, I am happy to confirm that it's absolutely true what they say: real life is so much more stimulating than fiction.

The personal stories in this book are drawn from a variety of life experiences, plus some I've heard from friends (which I do, indeed, believe). After studying history in college, my subsequent adventures have included: driving a truck for a small Boston warehouse; traveling Europe on a shoestring budget for three-and-a-half years (learning languages and working odd jobs in Sweden, Switzerland, and Greece); teaching English for three years as a volunteer in Thailand; running an emergency room as a nurse practitioner for five years in remote Appalachia; and training health workers for four years as a volunteer card-carrying missionary in El Salvador's villages and urban shantytowns. (The latter was during the country's civil war; my expatriate medical group arranged residency and work permits through the politically neutral Catholic Church. I'm not at all Catholic, but I did carry an ID card declaring me to be a "lay missionary.")

Since 1990, I've become domestic. I now practice in a health center serving low-income immigrants in San Francisco's Latino community. Since both my wife and I work part time, we were able to share childcare once Rebecca was born in 1993, then Leah in 1997 (a week before I turned fifty). I loved going to playgrounds, then school shows, violin recitals, summer camps, family trips (my second childhood of sorts). Now, I try to remain productive in our empty nest, assiduously avoiding third childhood by reading the news and writing.

As long as I still have my mental powers and finger dexterity, what better time than now to jot down the variety of odd stories I've been drawn to over the years (well, type them up)? My goal is partly to inform, partly to evoke head-shaking amazement, and of course, to generate laughter. I've actively sought out reasons to laugh ever since childhood. It's a good thing, too, as laughter has a variety of health benefits. It can ameliorate pain, reduce stress hormones, increase neurotransmitters that relieve depression, and release endorphins, our natural opioids, a little like sex does. Plainly put, laughter feels great (duh!).

Most selections are short, the longest reads in under three minutes. Some names are changed to protect the perps. I've included sources for the stories I've come across in newspapers, but a few escape me. (If you are especially keen to find an original article, just type a few keywords into your favorite search engine and you shall have your answer—voilà.) Those from the British press were found by my daughter Rebecca in London, studying Shakespeare, who, I'm proud to say, often shares my sense of humor. If any of my writing seems like it could be a pun, it's surely intended. The photographs, capturing absurdity in real life, are all mine.

There's no particular order to the stories, though we'll start with topics of life and death.

Life and Death

"Pale Death with impartial step knocks at the door of the poor man's hut, and at the gates of kings' palaces."

—Horace, *Odes*

"We should mourn men at their birth, and not their death."

—Montesquieu, *Persian Letters*

"Many people die at twenty-five, and aren't buried until seventy-five."

—Benjamin Franklin

1. Life After Death
(Same as Before)

In 2019, a sixty-one-year-old man serving life imprisonment in Iowa argued in court that his sentence should be over. The fellow had a major seizure in prison, during which he suffered a cardiac arrest, from which he was successfully resuscitated. As such, he insisted he had died, however briefly, and therefore his sentence had been served. He should now be free to leave.

Judge said "no."

See: Nicholas Bogel-Burroughs, "A Prisoner Who Briefly Died Argues that He's Served His Life Sentence," *New York Times*, November 8, 2019, https://www.nytimes.com/2019/11/08/us/prisoner-dies-life-sentence.html (accessed December 27, 2022).

2. Life After Death
(Sadly, Different from Before)

A man's wife died after a long illness on December 28, 2015. On March 3, 2016, he discovered his ATM card no longer worked. A call to his bank revealed why—the man was reported to have died, curiously, on the same date as his wife. His account had thus been frozen. Soon after, a pharmacy refused to refill a prescription because his health insurance had been cancelled. Hospitals refused to see him at scheduled appointments. Social Security sent his estate a letter of condolence, then not only stopped payments, but tried to retrieve automatic deposits that had been made to his bank for January and February.

Death certificates are issued at the state level, then uploaded electronically to Social Security's "Death Master File." Errors may occur about a thousand times a month, usually due to typos while entering social security numbers. Although the bureaucratic mess occurs quickly, undoing it is not nearly as efficient. Our gentleman was informed that long lines of live people were waiting in front of him.

Try not to let it happen to you (LOL) (meaning both "laugh out loud" and "lots of luck").

See: Thomas H. Lee, "Coming Back from the Dead," *New England Journal of Medicine*, 375, no. 6, 507-9 (2016),

3. Defying the Odds

During a conversation after the 2018 mass shooting in Thousand Oaks, California (near Malibu), a colleague expressed her amazement to me that one of the survivors had also been present at the mass shooting in Las Vegas a year earlier. I said if she was impressed by that guy's luck, wait until she reads the 2010 obituary for Tsutomu Yamaguchi, who passed away in Japan at age ninety-three. At twenty-nine, he was on a business trip to Hiroshima on August 6, 1945, when the first atomic bomb was dropped. Less than two miles from ground zero, he suffered burns and ruptured ear drums. He then returned home the next day to Nagasaki, just in time for the second bomb to land there, on August 9.

Mr. Yamaguchi was the only officially acknowledged "double A-bomb survivor," although there may have been about 165 others. He recovered fully, and as he got older, became more involved in movements against nuclear weapons. He was very philosophical about his experience, noting that, having escaped death twice, "Everything that follows is a bonus."

See: Mark McDonald, "Tsutomu Yamaguchi, Survivor of Two Atomic Blasts, Dies at 93," *New York Times*, January 6, 2010, https://www.nytimes.com/2010/01/07/world/asia/07yamaguchi.html (accessed December 27, 2022).

4. Saving Yourself in Nuclear War

For those who weren't born yet or are too young to remember, during the 1950s the possibility of nuclear war with the Soviet Union hovered constantly over Americans' heads (metaphor intentional). To prepare our country, the Federal Civil Defense Administration created a series of films titled *Duck and Cover* to educate schoolkids what to do in the event of an atomic bomb attack. We learned how to protect ourselves by ducking under school desks or, if outside, covering ourselves with a blanket or newspaper. According to the films, these measures could prevent dangers like "a really bad sunburn."

I guess we felt reassured enough, since I don't remember growing up in constant fear, though I do recall some concern during the Cuban Missile Crisis of 1962. But I was older then, so I could comprehend a bit more (but didn't carry a blanket or newspaper around). Enjoy the short clip cited below (search Google: "duck and cover macdonald"). If you want to hear my favorite song about nuclear annihilation, google "Tom Lehrer We Will All Go Together."

See: US Office of Civil Defense, "Duck and Cover," *Library of Congress*, Macdonald (J. Fred and Leslie W.) Collection, 1951, Library of Congress Control Number 2022604365, https://www.loc.gov/item/mbrs01836081/ (accessed December 24, 2002).

5. Back from the Dead

"Cryopreservation," aka "Cryonics," is the process of freezing an embalmed body (or just the brain), storing it for however long it might take scientists to find a cure for whatever caused death, then bringing the person back to life. The process may sound iffy (to say the least), but proponents argue that even a remote possibility of coming back to life beats the alternative. Companies offering cryopreservation can be found primarily in the US, Russia, Australia, and China. On average, the process costs around $200,000. Colloquially, the facilities have been called freezatoria (singular, freezatorium).

In America, most purchasers are men. In Russia, the gender balance is closer to fifty-fifty, since men there apparently want their mothers frozen with them. Americans, however, are more likely to pay for pets to be their cryopreserved companions so as not to wake up all alone.

The legitimately scientific Society of Cryobiology, which studies effects of low temperature on living tissue in procedures like in vitro fertilization, once banned its members from participating in cryopreservation. One of its presidents has compared cryonics to "believing you can turn hamburger back into a cow," while another opined it leaned more toward "fraud than either faith or science." The COVID pandemic has crimped the cryonics industry significantly since hospitals aren't eager to let people whom they might view as quacks fiddle around in ICUs.

Lawsuits against cryopreservation companies are not unusual and are often brought by relatives who balk at the loss of the cost, a significant potential inheritance. I recall a cartoon from the 1960s: woman in tears, cop at the door, who says, "There's been a power outage at the freezatorium, and … your husband spoiled."

See: Peter Wilson, "The Cryonics Industry Would Like to Give You the Past Year, and Many More, Back," *New York Times*, June 26, 2021, https://www.nytimes.com/2021/06/26/style/cryonics-freezing-bodies.html (accessed December 27, 2022).

6. Remind Me I'm Getting Old

When I turned fifty, I began to receive invitations to join the AARP. Not long after, the Neptune Society sought me out—the organization promoting affordable cremation. Neptune was the Roman version of Poseidon, god of the sea, which is ostensibly what people might choose as their final destination (see below). Then, I got a letter from the Hemlock Society, the right-to-die organization established in 1980 to legalize assisted suicide. The ancient Greek philosopher Socrates drank a slurry of the hemlock tree's poisonous root when executed by Athens in 399 BC. The Hemlock Society itself died (went defunct) in 2003.

Tragically, in 1997, a California pilot killed himself after the local sheriff found thousands of boxes of ashes in a storage locker and an airplane hangar. Apparently, the pilot had collected tens of thousands of dollars from families expecting him to scatter their loved ones' remains over the Pacific.

See: "Pilot Sought for Unstrewn Ashes Is Found Dead," *New York Times*, June 26, 1997, A20, https://www.nytimes.com/1997/06/26/us/pilot-sought-for-unstrewn-ashes-is-found-dead.html (accessed October 28, 2023).

7. Japan Has Fewer Centenarians than Thought

Japan is famous for having more people living past a hundred than any other country. Lots of explanations for this achievement have been offered, from lifestyle differences to diet to genetics. But in 2010, it was discovered that almost a quarter of a million centenarians hadn't really made it that far at all—many families simply never reported their relatives' deaths in order to keep collecting their pensions. At least one well-aged "person" was found mummified in bed for thirty years while the checks kept coming.

See: Martin Fackler, "Japan's Elderly Count Was Off by 234,000," *New York Times*, September 10, 2010, https://www.nytimes.com/2010/09/11/world/asia/11japan. html?_r=0 (accessed December 27, 2022).

Authority:
Rules, Rules, Rules

"Any fool can make a rule, And any fool will mind it."
—Henry David Thoreau, *Journal #14*

"Nothing strengthens authority as much as silence."
—Leonardo da Vinci

"Wherever there is a man who exercises authority, there is a man who resists authority."
—Oscar Wilde, *The Soul of Man under Socialism*

8. The Good Terrorist

In Somalia, which is 99 percent Muslim and among the world's poorest and most war-torn countries, the Al Qaeda-allied terrorist group Al-Shabaab battles back and forth daily with the government's police and military. Its atrocities targeting civilians are barbaric, and in areas it controls, the group has banned movies, music, and humanitarian aid groups, among other things. In 2018, it added another prohibited item: plastic bags, out of concern for the environment. Suicide bombings and assassinations of course continue, but plastic bags are forbidden because Al-Shabaab determined they "pose a serious threat to the well-being of humans and animals alike."

How nice and considerate.

See: Rukmini Callimachi, "Al Qaeda-Backed Terrorist Group Has a New Target: Plastic Bags," *New York Times*, July 4, 2018, https://www.nytimes.com/2018/07/04/world/africa/somalia-shabab-plastic-bags.html (accessed December 27, 2022).

9. Carpool Lanes

We've probably all seen those people driving with inflatable dummies in their passenger seats in order to sneak into carpool lanes. Well, in 2006, a pregnant woman in Arizona tried to assert her right to drive there with the argument that she had another passenger inside (her). She fought the ticket, but the judge didn't buy it, and fined her court costs as well.

Things may have changed since Roe v. Wade's reversal, depending on which state you're in. A Texas judge threw out a similar case in 2022, acquitting the woman. So be mindful if you're pregnant and driving cross-country, and find yourself tempted to declare other less-obvious "passengers."

In Las Vegas, a funeral home van driver claimed his four corpses in the back were occupants, to no avail. And in 2013, a man in Marin County, California, argued that the articles of incorporation for his business, which lay on the front seat, warranted "personhood" (shades of the Supreme Court's decision *Citizens United*?). That didn't fly either, and to make matters worse, the paperwork wasn't even seat belted.

See: Brian Dakss, "Pregnant Woman Loses HOV Lane Case," *CBS News*, January 12, 2006, https://www.cbsnews.com/news/pregnant-woman-loses-hov-lane-case/ (accessed December 26, 2022).

Vanessa Romo, "Pregnant Woman Who Claimed Her Fetus Was an HOV Lane Passenger Gets Another Ticket," *NPR*, September 2, 2022, https://www.npr.org/2022/09/02/1120628973/pregnant-woman-dallas-fetus-hov-lane-passenger-ticket (accessed December 27, 2022).

David Montero, "A Tip from the Highway Patrol: Carpooling with the dead Doesn't Mean You Get to Use the HOV Lane," *Los Angeles Times*, July 2, 2019, https://www.latimes.com/nation/la-na-hearse-dead-body-hov-lane-20190702-story.html (accessed December 27, 2022).

Justin Burton, "Corporation Not Person in Carpool Lanes," *SFGate*, Jan. 8, 2013, https://www.sfgate.com/bayarea/article/Corporation-not-person-in-carpool-lanes-4173366.php (accessed December 27, 2022).

10. "Anti"-Corruption?

A participant in Ireland's 2022 Dublin Marathon was caught using public transportation for part of the course. Interestingly—or worryingly—he happened to be an off-duty member of the Garda's (national police force) anti-corruption unit. The runner apologized and returned the t-shirt and medal he received for having completed the race. As of press time, Police Headquarters intended to investigate the matter, saying the officer would be asked to explain and be "offered support if deemed necessary," though it did add that there may be implications regarding ongoing service in the anti-corruption unit.

See: Paul Reynolds, "Garda Accused of Using Luas to Complete Dublin Marathon," *RTÉ News*, November 11, 2022, https://www.rte.ie/news/ireland/2022/1111/1335617-garda-marathon/ (accessed December 24, 2022). [translations: "garda" = "police officer; "gardaí" is the plural; "Luas" = Dublin's light rail system]

11. No Fun at Disney World

Two strangers coincidentally visited Disney World on October 20, 2022. One hailed from Brooklyn and was on the lam after scamming almost $150,000 from COVID relief programs through identity theft. The other happened to be a federal agent assigned to the case. The agent recognized the fugitive from photographs and alerted park security, who contacted local police to arrest the man. A Florida court prepared to free him on bail, but a New York federal judge overruled, citing the fellow's abundant use of false identities.

The lesson? Identity theft is no Mickey Mouse adventure.

See: Ramon Antonio Vargas, "Man on Run from Fraud Charges Arrested After Officer Spots Him at Disney World," *Guardian*, November 6, 2022, https://www.theguardian.com/us-news/2022/nov/06/florida-disney-world-fugutive-fraud-case (accessed December 27, 2022).

12. Read the Policy

An attorney friend told me how she represented an insurance company on appeal that went as far as the state Supreme Court. A man had purchased an accident insurance policy that specifically excluded "injuries sustained while riding a motorcycle," but never bought the additional add-on to cover them. He later had an accident on his motorcycle, and the insurer denied payment because of the exclusion. The man, however, insisted he should be covered because his injuries were sustained not while riding the vehicle but after being thrown onto the ground.

Amazingly enough, two lower courts ruled in his favor. The Supreme Court, which happened to be fractiously divided in most cases, voted unanimously in favor of the insurance company. Not that I tend to side with big business, but common sense does deserve some deference in legal decisions.

In another strange case for the annals of insurance, in 2022 Geico Insurance was ordered to pay over $5 million to a woman who sued a consensual sex partner for infecting her with genital warts when they had sex in the back seat of his car. The Missouri Court of Appeals upheld her local court's verdict, which, I guess, considered this a sort of car accident.

Geico didn't even get to argue initially, since the original agreement was reached through arbitration, which it hadn't been informed about. Interestingly, human papillomavirus (HPV, the cause of genital warts) can lie dormant inside you for years before becoming obvious. Before the vaccine, virtually everyone who'd ever had sex was infected with one strain or another, so it was almost impossible to tell who you caught it from.

Some strains of HPV cause cancer, but those strains can't be seen. So, if you have nasty-looking genital warts, at least be relieved to know that what you have won't hurt you. But of course, you might have other invisible warts which could. Only the woman here could be tested for the latter, not the man.

Geico appealed to a federal court.

See: Timothy Bella, "She Got an STD During Car Sex. Now, Geico Could Pay Her $5.2 Million," *Washington Post*, June 9, 2022, https://www.washingtonpost.com/nation/2022/06/09/geico-std-car-sex-missouri-insurance/ (accessed December 27, 2022).

Asha Gilbert, "Geico Ordered to Pay $5.2 Million to Woman Who Contracted STD During Sex in Insured Vehicle," *USA Today*, June 10, 2022 / updated June 13, 2022, https://www.usatoday.com/story/money/2022/06/10/geico-std-law-suit-missouri/7578871001/ (accessed December 31, 2022).

13. I Have to Pee

After college, I worked for two years at a Boston warehouse, driving a truck delivering electrical supplies to local construction sites, enjoying city life on my own, and saving money to travel. My first supervisor was a big jolly man named John M. It was some time before I learned about his chronic pain from the shrapnel he'd retained from the Korean War; you'd never have realized it. I recall two of his bits of wisdom.

One was delivered the Monday he announced he'd been to the dog races over the weekend and had won $1,500. Upon leaving the track, he swore he'd never gamble again. Why? So he could always tell himself that he came out ahead. I didn't gamble, but I found this philosophy enlightening.

More useful to me, though, was his clever advice on how we workers should cope with a pesky overseer. Business had been going badly at the warehouse, and our boss sold out to a competitor. My coworkers and I were informed we had two weeks to pack up all the stock to ship out and then we'd lose our jobs. That by itself was a downer. But the new owner sent his own man, Frank, to make sure we weren't slacking on the job or stealing stuff. He hovered incessantly and was an absolute pain.

John M. advised us to go to the bathroom. "Excuse yourself to go pee. Each in turn." After me, Wally had to pee; when he returned, Billy felt the urge; then Sam; then I had to go again. And on it went. Nobody could begrudge us the need to respond to bodily functions, not even Frank. He went nuts and soon disappeared, leaving us alone to do our jobs.

So, if you're ever stuck at a workplace with a superior breathing down your neck, just go pee. It can work out great. One thing's for sure: you'll no longer be pissed. A great relief.

14. Learning from Error?

In the early 1990s, an attorney I know had just begun practicing at a prestigious firm when she was assigned to represent an elderly lady *pro bono*. Her client was about to lose her house to a couple of sleazy real estate lawyers who had hoodwinked her into signing a contract she hadn't fully understood. My friend had no real defense except for a technicality: the lawyers were supposed to alert the lady to impending foreclosure by two certified letters, and they had only produced the signed return receipt for one.

An hour before court, my friend received a fax with the second certified receipt. She was furious; now, with no time left, the case seemed hopeless. She held the two faxes up, glared at them, and proceeded to notice that the signatures were identical. She compared them side-to-side, up-and-down—identical signatures. Obviously, the real estate sleazes couldn't find the second receipt, so they photocopied the first and doctored the date.

My friend immediately called her firm's handwriting expert, who opined, "Identical signatures? Impossible." She promptly faxed back, "Doubt authenticity. Will settle on our terms only, unconditionally." The elderly lady got to keep her home, and my friend even collected attorney fees from the two lawyers. After the case was over and done, she reported them to the state bar association, which merely issued a reprimand (the proverbial "slap on the wrist").

Several years later, a prospective client approached my friend, asking her to represent him on some case. She asked who had recommended her, only to discover it was one of the two sleazy lawyers! Apparently, they were impressed by how clever she was. This might have been the ultimate compliment. Lest there be any perceived conflict of interest, she declined the new case.

15. Birds Are Grounded; Ferrets and Pigs, Too

Airlines have firm limits. In 2018, a woman struggled for six hours to arrange for her comfort animal, a peacock, to accompany her on a United Airlines flight from Newark to Los Angeles before bailing out and traveling by road instead. This might seem unfair, since a turkey had been allowed to fly from Seattle to Salt Lake City two years prior. But United said the peacock didn't meet guidelines for weight and size ("size" must have included the tail).

Ferrets are also non grata. One escaped from the passenger's purse while she was asleep and scurried around the plane amidst laughter and shrieks. Canada's two national airlines mandate that a comfort animal be kept in a soft carrier stowed under the seat, lest it wind up a projectile during an emergency, and ferrets are especially problematic because they could chew their way through a soft carrier. A plethora of ferret-lovers circulated a petition in protest.

In 2014, a pet pig squealed and pooped in a plane just before takeoff. It, and its owner, were taken off.

See: "'Emotional Support Peacock' Barred from United Airlines Plane," *BBC News*, January 31, 2018, https://www.bbc.com/news/world-us-canada-42880690 (accessed April 23, 2023).

Darcy Wintonyk and Lynda Steele, "Ferret Owners Petition to Allow Pets on Flights," *CTV News*, December 14, 2012, https://bc.ctvnews.ca/ferret-owners-petition-to-allow-pets-on-flights-1.1075272 (accessed April 23, 2023).

"Ferrets on a Plane," *Sky Floor*, April 23, 2001, https://www.theskyfloor.com/ferrets-on-a-plane/ (accessed April 23, 2023).

16. Pay if You Puke

To attract customers during the pandemic, several restaurants in the San Francisco Bay Area began offering unlimited mimosas with brunch. The strategy was successful, beyond belief in several senses. Some afficionados drank to the point of vomiting, in the restrooms, or even at the table. This proved understandably disquieting to nearby patrons attempting to enjoy their meals, as well as to staff who had to clean up.

Some establishments posted signs threatening a $50 cleaning fee. Another designated an employee as "mimosa fairy" to circulate among tables refilling drinks, simultaneously surveying for customers too intoxicated to hold their liquor. Servers had all passed a mandatory state exam for employees serving alcohol.

In ancient Rome, the philosopher Seneca complained how the wealthy would "vomit that they may eat, and eat that they may vomit." One method was to tickle the throat with a feather. This, by the way, was not pathological bulimia, but simple gluttony to an extreme.

In the early 1980s, a patient came to my Kentucky emergency room for vomiting. I asked him how many times he had vomited, and he replied, "eleven," which seemed unusually exact. I inquired how much alcohol he had drunk: "eleven beers." He had thrown up after the first one, drank another to calm his stomach, vomited again, and so on, eleven times in all. To me, this suggested a distinct lack of insight, though it is amazing the extent that people struggle to convince themselves.

See: Jessica Yadegaran, "Bay Area Restaurants Institute Penalty for Brunch Vomiters," *SF Gate*, October 8, 2023, https://www.sfgate.com/food/article/bay-area-restaurants-throwing-up-brunch-18411628.php (accessed October 9, 2023).

17. Kids versus Lawyers

Sometime around 2010, a tree fell on Strawberry Hill, an island in the middle of Blue Heron Lake in San Francisco's beautiful Golden Gate Park (formerly Stow Lake, renamed in 2024 after discovering Stow had been a nineteenth-century virulent antisemite). The downed trunk is about thirty feet long, stripped now of all bark, with a few protruding branches to climb on, which are at most six feet off the ground. It's a wonderful, unplanned play structure for children.

But when the tree first fell, a park worker told me, the parks department ordered them to chop it up, as they do with all fallen trees. This one must have smelled of liability, lest somebody fall off and get hurt. But the workers protested, "Children love it." Surprisingly (to me, at least), supervisors relented, and let it stay. Nothing adverse has happened to date.

Kids 1, Lawyers 0.

Actually, on rare occasions, people get seriously injured or killed by falling pine cones. Even if they are just half a pound, they do fall from on high. Falling branches are worse. This usually happens when it's windy, but can also occur on calm days if the branch or the entire tree has rotted enough. The wood offers a few seconds of warning with its telltale creak. My advice? If you hear it, don't look straight up because you'll never have time to flee. Instead, run off looking up but ahead of you, to make sure your destination is safe. Disclosure: I've never had to try this, but it seems logical.

18. Bumper-to-Bumper

I'm pretty good at maneuvering in and out of tight parking spaces. But one day I went out to my car, parallel parked across our driveway, found cars in front and in back, both literally touching my bumper. There was absolutely not an inch on either side to jockey. But weirdest of all, one car had lots of room in front of it—no need at all to have backed up right against my bumper!

I needed to drive to work in a few hours, which would have been impossible. So, I called the local police precinct's non-emergency line. They said they couldn't tow the cars nor do anything if they were legally parked, which they were. But I could report them as "hit-and-run," since they were touching my bumper ("hit") and the drivers had left ("run").

As annoyed and desperate as I was, that did seem excessive. And since the owner could have easily known whose car and house it was, the report may have gotten me a brick hurled through my front window. Fortunately, they drove off before I had to leave for work.

Hit-and-run ?!?!?!?

Society and Family: Friends and Foes

"In individuals, insanity is rare; but in groups, parties, nations, and epochs, it is the rule."

—Friedrich Nietzsche, *Beyond Good and Evil*

"If the misery of the poor be caused not by the laws of nature, but by our institutions, great is our sin."

—Charles Darwin, *Voyage of the Beagle*

"After a good dinner one can forgive anybody, even one's own relations."

—Oscar Wilde, *A Woman of No Importance*

19. The Klan Tries to Help Out

In 2001, the Missouri chapter of the KKK applied to participate in an "Adopt-A-Highway" program to clean up roadside trash. The state refused, and the Klan sued. The courts ruled in the Klan's favor, affirming they had the right to take part in the program. Down but not out, the state decided to rename that stretch of road the "Rosa Parks Highway." We can imagine the joy Rosa and anyone else might have had as men in white hoods stooped down to serve her. But it never materialized; the Klan backed out, probably out of laziness.

See: David Mikkelson, "Did Missouri Rename a Highway Adopted by the KKK After Rosa Parks?", *Snopes*, December 3, 2001, https://www.snopes.com/fact-check/kkk-highway-renamed-after-rosa-parks/ (accessed 12/24/2022).

20. Religious Denominations

I landed my first job as a nurse practitioner in 1980, at a nonprofit clinic in Eastern Kentucky. That part of Appalachia was, and likely still is, one of the poorest in the country. Its foothills were settled in the eighteenth century by Scotch-Irish pioneers who never continued on to the Great Plains or farther west. Many may have been fugitives seeking relative seclusion. The area had no economic potential except farming corn on slopes (and brewing moonshine) until coal was discovered around 1900, mined by out-of-state companies who exploited the land and workers for profit. The spoken dialect was said to be closer to 1776 English than anything in Britain today; isolated cultures don't tend to change over time.

Most people belonged to mainstream Protestant denominations, but a fair number worshiped in offshoot congregations and even sects. Rare ones handled snakes to prove their faith, inspired by a New Testament passage in the Gospel of Mark (search for "snake-handling churches CNN video" for a five-minute clip, or "holy ghost snake handlers" for longer ones). Anyone could proclaim themselves pastor and establish a "church." Each tiny valley, or hollow (pronounced "holler"), would have one or two churches for the large extended families living there. Pastors might compete. One once burned down another's church.

Our clinic was governed by a volunteer community board. Its president was a very friendly man in his forties, a pastor at a local Church of Christ, which is a loose collection of independent congregations around the world. One of their main tenets in common is a prohibition on playing instruments at services (from a passage in Ephesians), but that was all I knew. Attempting to show an interest, I asked him, "What does your denomination believe in?"

His brow furrowed as he replied, "We're not a 'denomination.'" In other words, they were the "Truth." I should have known better than to bring up religion.

See also: "Mountaineers and Rangers," *NPS History Electronic Library & Archive*, http://npshistory.com/publications/usfs/region/8/history/intro.htm#:~:text=The%20early%20settlers%20were%20primarily,Palatinate%20(west%20Rhine)%20Germans (accessed September 3, 2023).

21. Rotten Luck

A doctor friend of mine described how, while he was away on vacation, a blind patient of his sought a note for getting out of jury duty. The gentleman made an appointment with one of my friend's colleagues who himself happened to be blind. The blind doctor was offended by the thought. "Excuse? No way! I can offer a request for reasonable accommodation, but not a total excuse."

The poor man really picked the wrong day to get out of jury duty.

22. How Many Half-Siblings Might You Have?

This is dangerous. My daughter knew a girl who, after starting college, happened to strike up a friendship with another girl. Over time, they both realized how much they seemed to have in common, and everyone else noticed how much they looked alike. Their connection turned out to be more than coincidence: they eventually discovered through their parents that they'd been sired by the same sperm donor.

Some men seem to take joy in donating as much sperm as they can. Some fertility specialists have even been found to have been implanting their own in patients, completely unbeknownst to the latter. Headlines suggest that this deception may be rampant. A friend in London once told me about a doctor who had been nick-named "Semen Demon."

Is there an epidemic of inbreeding on the horizon? Stay tuned!

See: Christina Burke, "Fertility Doctor Sued for Using Own Sperm in Treating Patients," *PET*, September 21, 2020, https://www.bionews.org.uk/page_152002 (accessed December 24, 2022).

23. Who Are You Named For?

My favorite ancient Greek myth is the one about Cassandra. As the story goes, the god Apollo wanted to sleep with her. He offered her the gift of prophesy, which she readily accepted, but then broke her promise—she wouldn't go to bed. Apollo was angry, but he couldn't undo her new powers, so he added a curse on top of them: yes, Cassandra would always be able to foretell the future, but nobody would ever believe her! Cassandra went mad. Modern psychiatry even speaks informally of the "Cassandra Syndrome" (or "Ongoing Traumatic Relationship Syndrome"), describing the frustration and invisibility felt by partners or children of emotionally numb people with Asperger's Syndrome, when others don't believe their unique distress.

I haven't met many women named Cassandra, but whenever I do, I always wonder whether to ask if they know where their name came from. I never do.

See: "The Myth of Cassandra," *Greek Myths and Greek Mythology*, https://www.greekmyths-greekmythology.com/the-myth-of-cassandra/ (accessed December 24, 2022).

Sarah Cook Ruggera, "Cassandra Syndrome," October 7, 2018, https://couplescounselorsandiego.com/cassandra-syndrome/ (accessed December 24, 2022).

24. What to Call Mom-in-Law

In the early 1980s, a friend married the man whom she'd been dating for several years. At the wedding, his mother, whom my friend had always called "Jessica," announced how now, as part of the family, she wanted to be called "Nana." That sounded just a little too goofy for my friend, who could never quite bring herself to do it. For the next twenty-five or so years, until Jessica/Nana passed away in old age, my friend had to contrive roundabout ways and linguistic contortions to speak without offending her mother-in-law.

25. South Korea Feels the Pinch
(Women, Beware!)

Many South Korean men went bonkers in 2021 over a major convenience store chain's ad for camping products. The picture featured a tent and campfire in a nighttime forest, with a hand reaching for a steaming-hot sausage. How horrible ...

It seems that in 2015, a now-defunct feminist website had used a similar pinching symbol for its logo to ridicule the size of men's penises. The image stuck, at least in the minds of many men who wailed in such protest that the chain, GS25, apologized profusely, disciplined the female ad designer, and demoted several executives.

The uproar continued, however, as irate men dug up other ads with similar images for products including a credit card, Starbucks espresso, and the COVID vaccine.

In light of all the drama, perhaps it's unsurprising that South Korea ranked number one in a Pew 2022 survey of conflict between the sexes. The *Economist* invariably considers it to have the worst work environment for women among all thirty-eight countries in the intergovernmental Organization for Economic Co-operation and Development (OECD). Either way, women who visit there best mind their fingers.

See: Hawon Jung, "The Little Symbol Triggering Men in South Korea's Gender War," *New York Times*, July 30, 2021, https://www.nytimes.com/2021/07/30/opinion/international-world/korea-emoji-feminism-misogyny.html (accessed January 23, 2023).

Yim Hyun-su, "Retailers Accused of Being 'Man-Haters' Over Gesture," *Korean Herald*, May 4, 2021, http://www.koreaherald.com/view.php?ud=20210504000923 (accessed January 23, 2023).

Laura Silver, "Most Across 19 Countries See Strong Partisan Conflicts in Their Society, Especially in South Korea and the U.S.," *Pew Research Center*, November 16, 2022, https://www.pewresearch.org/fact-tank/2022/11/16/most-across-19-countries-see-strong-partisan-conflicts-in-their-society-especially-in-south-korea-and-the-u-s/ (accessed March 20, 2023).

26. Her Forlorn Middle Initial

My mother was born Malvina Sternfield on Valentine's Day in 1917. So named, she became a nurse and served in the army during World War II. Upon marrying my father, George Leiner, in 1946, she changed her name to Malvina S. Leiner—the "S." for her maiden name—and used that to obtain a driver's license, sign my birth certificate, work in hospitals, get a passport, collect social security, and, above all, always pay taxes.

But in the early 1990s she hit a roadblock.

When she attempted to renew her passport long after its expiration, the US State Department required an original birth certificate. That document, to her amazement, had her first name miswritten as "Melvine." Apparently, the obstetrician who delivered her was either indifferent or sloppy. Her immigrant parents never noticed.

Despite my mom's protests and supporting documents such as army discharge papers and marriage license, the bureaucrats were unrelenting. However, they did note that although "Melvine" was a mandatory inclusion, it could be represented as a middle initial. As such, her new passport was issued under "Malvina M. Leiner."

When my mom moved to San Francisco to be near her grand-children after my father died, I tried filling out the form for a California ID card as simply "Malvina Leiner." But the Department of Motor Vehicles copied verbatim from her passport. For the next eleven years until she passed away at age ninety-six, she was known to our bureaucracy as "Malvina M."

There's a happy ending, though. Her tombstone at the Veterans Administration's Calverton National Cemetery is, indeed, engraved "Malvina S. Leiner."

27. NYC Can Really Be a Jungle

I n 2003, a New York City resident showed up at a hospital ER having been bitten by a "pit bull." His docs, however, were suspicious of the size and characteristics of the bite. As they began questioning him further, the patient fled, and staff alerted the NYPD. At the man's residence, neighbors complained to the cops about a persistent, strong smell of urine.

The police sawed a hole in the door and threaded in a video camera, stunned to see a tiger. They called for back-up. A sharpshooter rappelled from the roof, opened a window, and hit the animal with tranquilizer darts.

It turned out that the tiger, Ming, had been living for two years on the fifth floor of the spacious Harlem apartment building, along with other exotic animals. His owner had acquired him as an eight-week-old baby, who of course, eventually grew to over 400 pounds. Fortunately, the story has a happy ending: Ming was sent to an animal conservancy in Ohio, where he lived until his death in 2019, age nineteen.

Someone interviewed by the *New York Times* said, "Only in New York." Another was concerned that a "city cat won't make it in the country … no jazz, no hip-hop. He's going to miss the Harlem Renaissance." Fair enough.

See: Alan Feuer and Jason George, "Police Subdue Tiger in Harlem Apartment," *New York Times*, October 5, 2003, https://www.nytimes.com/2003/10/05/nyregion/police-subdue-tiger-in-harlem-apartment.html (accessed December 25, 2022).

Corey Kilgannon, "A 425-Pound Tiger Living in a Harlem Apartment? Yes, It Happened," *New York Times*, April 20, 2020, https://www.nytimes.com/2020/04/18/nyregion/ming-tiger-harlem-nyc.html (accessed December 25, 2022).

28. Not on Facebook!

In 2017, my friends Daniel and Lily attended her cousin Jack's wedding in Texas. Jack was marrying a local professor, who grew up in a wealthy Mexican family. The celebration was large and the reception lavish, with plenty of sumptuous food and all sorts of dancing. A lot of people were dressed formally and many took a lot of pictures. Daniel took pictures, too, and posted a few on Facebook.

The next morning, Jack's new wife called, steaming mad. "How dare you post pictures of my family? Who gave you the right?" Perplexed, Daniel duly apologized, not wanting to create a family rift.

When I heard the story, I immediately realized the only possible explanation. Who would come from a wealthy Mexican family and not want her relatives' pictures disseminated, other than the child of a major cartel figure? Daniel and Lily nodded silently when I suggested this might be the case, and that was that.

I searched Google a bit but couldn't find anything about the lives of children of drug lords. There must be quite a few. How privy are they to their parents' work? Are they all-out supportive, or do they have mixed feelings? Could we ever even find out?

A friend recently described how her high school daughter was best buddies with a Mexican girl who'd been sent to study in the United States "so that she wouldn't get kidnapped." Her family was rich. My friend had major misgivings, because as friendly and polite as the girl was, she seemed to lie a lot. Her stories kept changing about completely inconsequential things. It seemed like she was unconsciously on guard and determined that nobody should ever learn anything about her.

If she were your kid's best friend, would you let your child visit the family in Mexico?

29. Only in America

While working in El Salvador from 1986 to 1990 during its civil war, my expatriate medical buddies and I would often listen to broadcasts from the left-wing guerrillas' clandestine *Radio Venceremos* ("Victory"). They were a mix of propaganda and news items that were an alternative to what we'd hear on government stations. Who knows how true their information was, but at least it was different.

In May 1987, the rebels reported on an international story. That month, former US Senator Gary Hart, then the leading Democratic candidate for the following year's presidential election, suspended his campaign due to media exposés about an extramarital affair. Radio Venceremos reported something like, "Today in the United States, presidential candidate Gary Hart got caught having an affair and dropped out of the race. Colonel Garcia sleeps with his secretary, and he hasn't quit. Defense Minister Hernandez cheats around with General Perez's wife, and he's still in office." After a few more commentaries on other military officers' and government officials' sex lives, the guerrillas concluded, "Poor Gary Hart."

This would never have happened in Europe. The public there practically expects high-ups to have affairs, both men and women. In 2020, a candidate for mayor of Paris resigned after a sexting video surfaced. That kind of resignation had never occurred before in France. An enormous reaction ensued from the far-left to the far-right but not about the scandal itself; people were outraged about the video's newsworthiness. One political opponent asserted indignantly, "We are not electing a saint but the mayor of Paris." Commentators complained how French politics was becoming "Americanized."

See: John Lichfield, "The Not-So-Secret Sex Lives of French Politicians," *Politico*, February 18, 2020, https://www.politico.eu/article/the-not-so-secret-sex-lives-of-french-politicians-paris-mayoral-campaign-benjamin-griveaux-emmanuel-macron/ (accessed August 5, 2023).

30. Who Are the Customers?

Tiberon, California.

31. Thoughts on a Boo-Boo

Sharon lived across the apartment building's courtyard from me when we were in grad school in 1978. As a single mom in her mid-30s, she balanced academics with raising her three-year-old son, Ralphie. She told me one day how the boy had run to her crying, having dropped the toilet seat on his penis. There was no significant injury, but the boo-boo obviously hurt.

Ralphie asked his mom to kiss it, as she had done for all prior boo-boos elsewhere. Sharon declined, which was likely upsetting, though Ralphie recovered without physical or emotional scars.

If you were Sharon, would you have kissed the boo-boo?

32. On Parenting

O ur daughters were born in 1993 and 1997. There was no social media back then and very few people had access to what we then called the World Wide Web. Instead we had countless books and articles to rely on for parenting advice, but it didn't matter—we never read any of them. All through our lives my wife and I had always relied on common sense, which worked just fine. We just naturally prioritized love, laughter, and enthusiasm for whatever our daughters seemed drawn to.

I hear all sorts of parenting philosophies and usually just smile to myself. But I still recall the two instances I found unbelievable. The first day of preschool we noted a disproportionate number of boys in Rebecca's class and were then dismayed when one of the few girls soon left. A teacher explained how her parents had decided that, since she would be home-schooled come kindergarten, they didn't want her "to get too used to making friends."

Years later in a supermarket checkout line, the lady in front of me had a four-year-old in her shopping cart. I smiled at the girl, asked, "What's your name?" The mother advised me, "We teach her not to talk to strangers."

Oh, my.

While I never read any parenting books, I'm happy to recommend other books about kids. My go-to gift for pregnant friends is *Baby's First Tattoo*. It's from 2002, and I still give it. The small book is mostly to record key memories like "Baby's First Step," "Most Dirty Diapers in a Day," "Who Changes Them," "How Grandma Would Raise Baby Differently," "First Time After Birth We Had Sex," and so on. One page, "Do You Have a Gifted Child," offers insight with a list of fifteen questions, such as "Does your child act out?" and "Is your child easily bored?" The next page, "Does Your Child Have a Learning Disability," offers the same list of fifteen. The next, "Does Your Child Have ADHD," has the same questions again. And the page, "Do You Have a Pretty Much Average Kid"… you get the idea.

See: Jim Mullen, *Baby's First Tattoo: A Memory Book for Modern Parents* (New York: Simon & Shuster, 2002).

33. Fires and Smoke

Every summer or two here in San Francisco, smoke drifts in from terrible wildfires fifty to a hundred miles away. The sky may glow a gorgeous orange hue in the morning, which impressed us at first until we realized what it meant. To avoid the smoke, people tend to wear various kinds of masks, though only the N95 particulate respirator helps at all, and only if worn correctly (one strap above the ears, another below; won't work if you have a beard).

On occasion, I'd see someone wearing whatever mask proceed to pause, remove it … and then stick a cigarette in their mouth. (Take a deep breath.)

34. Amtrak Miscellany

Making fun of Amtrak may be low-hanging fruit, but here we go anyway. Long-distance trains stop every four or five hours, allowing passengers to get up and out and move around for ten to fifteen minutes. Amtrak courteously lets passengers know they are allowed to smoke in certain outdoor areas during the stop—what the train personnel call "fresh-air breaks."

Many years ago (pre-cell phones), I was taking an Amtrak home from New York City to the northern suburbs. It was late at night and I was very tired, but afraid of missing my stop. So I asked a passing conductor to wake me if I fell asleep. She replied, "Sure, but remind me." I managed to stay awake.

I recall a newspaper editorial cartoon from the 1970s after a week of three separate Amtrak accidents. It showed the proverbial evil man with curled mustache tying a maiden to the tracks ("Marry me or else"). She comments, "Oh, you're just tying me here—I was afraid you'd make me ride the train."

35. Disability Equality

In 1997, Mattel, Inc., introduced a new Barbie doll, Becky, in a wheelchair. Unfortunately, it couldn't fit through the door of Barbie's house, nor into its elevator. Instead of redesigning the house to allow accommodation, the company simply dumped Becky and discontinued the line. It took over another twenty years for Mattel to finally introduce new disabled dolls.

In 2020, American Girl's "Girl of the Year" was Joss, a doll that suffered from hearing loss. It took six years and over 145,000 signatures for them to come up with a disabled doll, after initially refusing. At the time, one young woman I know expressed surprise that all the other American Girl dolls could really hear.

See: Sarah Kim, "Why Mattel's Inclusion of Barbie Dolls with Disabilities Isn't Enough," *Forbes*, February 19, 2019, https://www.forbes.com/sites/sarah-kim/2019/02/19/barbie-dolls-with-disabiilities/?sh=323f00851319 (accessed December 26, 2022).

Shaun Heasley, "American Girl Introduces Doll with Disability," *Disability Scoop*, January 10, 2020, https://www.disabilityscoop.com/2020/01/10/american-girl-introduces-doll-with-disability/27632/ (accessed December 24, 2022).

36. Culture War in San Francisco?

A giant 100-foot cement cross sits upon San Francisco's Mt. Davidson, the highest peak in the city (maybe it's just a hill). It was erected in 1934, after several previous wooden crosses burned (were burned?) down. But in 1991, the American Civil Liberties Union, the American Jewish Federation, and Americans United for Separation of Church and State sued to have it removed from city property. The city chose to auction off the cross plus its fraction-of-an-acre parcel of land at its base. Two members of American Atheists sued up to the Supreme Court to prevent the sale, but the city won. San Francisco sold the bundle to the city's tiny Armenian community.

The Armenians promptly added a plaque, declaring the cross to be a commemoration of the 1915 Armenian genocide, when 1,500,000 people were murdered by the Ottoman Empire. That infuriated San Francisco's tiny Turkish community, members of whom (along with the local Turkish consulate) sued to remove the plaque. The Armenians won. The plaque got stolen but then replaced; I haven't heard of anything since.

Goes to show you can't please everyone—sometimes, not even *anyone*.

See: "History of the Cross," *Mt. Davidson Cross*, https://www.mountdavidson-cross.org/about-the-cross (accessed December 26, 2022).

"Lawsuit by Turks Against Armenia's Dismissed," *Asbarez*, January 26, 2004, https://asbarez.com/lawsuit-by-turks-against-armenias-dismissed/ (accessed December 26, 2022).

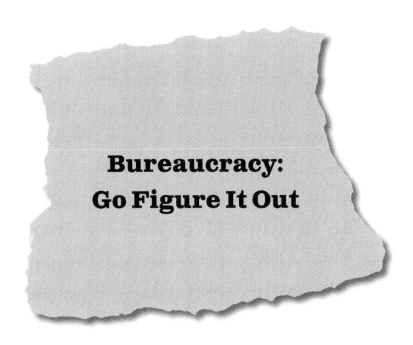

Bureaucracy: Go Figure It Out

"The chains that cuff humanity are made of office paper"
—Franz Kafka, *Diaries*

"Imagine all the contradictions, all possible incompatibilities, and you'll see them in the government, in the courts, in the churches, and the public scenes of this silly old nation."
—Voltaire, *Candide*

"Bureaucracy and social harmony are inversely proportional to each other."
—Leon Trotsky, *The Revolution Betrayed*

37. Vicious Cycle

A physician friend related how a man was brought to his emergency room by ambulance for chest pain. It had occurred after a stressful situation. Fortunately, the patient's tests were all normal, and the final diagnosis was "anxiety reaction."

Everything was fine until several months later … when the man received a big ambulance bill. He immediately got chest pain upon opening the envelope and called 911. My friend was on duty when the patient arrived this second time. What can you say?

38. Life and Death via Lottery

On December 1, 1969, the US military's Selective Service, commonly known as the Draft Board, held its first lottery since World War II. All previous exemptions were cancelled; until then, college students had been able to defer service, while those from more disadvantaged backgrounds made up the bulk of the military (and its deaths during Vietnam). The Draft Lottery sought to make dying in war fairer.

Fairer perhaps in that all men were treated equally (no women were drafted at the time), but not exactly. As one statistician described such a lottery, "There are two ways to go about it. You can be certain of being random by picking a table of random numbers, [which] can be found in just about any statistics textbook … Or you can have a show and use a fishbowl." The army opted for the latter.

Their process involved stuffing plastic capsules with papers bearing birthdates, combining them in a big container, and then picking capsules out one by one, all in public view. Appears simple enough, but one seemingly small detail was botched, ultimately having an enormous impact on who got picked.

First, capsules with birthdates from January first to thirty-first were placed in a box and pushed to one side. Then the February capsules were dropped in the empty half and mixed with January's. Next came March, and so on. As a result, January birthdates were mixed eleven times, but November's were only mixed twice, and December's just once.

The box was then emptied into a two-foot-deep bowl—which nobody stirred. Various people reached in to pick out capsules one by one in public view; predictably, young men with December birthdays wound up being disproportionately drafted. After the process was criticized, the military went on the defensive, with a captain arguing that the capsules were mixed even more while the box was being carried up and down stairs. Most people drawing picked from the top, though some did reach into the middle or bottom of the bowl.

Maybe all's not fair in love and war.

See: David E. Rosenbaum, "Statisticians Charge Draft Lottery Was Not Random," *New York Times*, January 4, 1970, https://www.nytimes.com/1970/01/04/archives/statisticians-charge-draft-lottery-was-not-random.html (accessed December 27, 2022).

39. Fancy Hiking Trail

I n the early 1980s, I backpacked seventy miles in Pennsylvania, I think it was along the Laurel Highlands Trail. It was a Cadillac of hiking trails: well-blazed, with shelters every five to ten miles equipped with fireplaces and stocked with wood. The shelters also provided latrines, and the latrines had disability-support transfer (grab) bars. For people who had backpacked in?!

I stopped at a ranger station along the way and inquired out of curiosity about the bars. The ranger explained that when the trail was initially designed, bureaucrats balked at the architect plans. A shelter was an official state facility, which by law had to meet certain accessibility standards. Hence architects added the transfer bars. I'm not sure how often they get used.

40. The Monday Before

In 1968, Congress, in its infinite wisdom, passed the "Monday before" law. The bill specified that if a holiday fell "on a weekday" it would be celebrated the Monday before in order to give Americans a three-day weekend. The law took effect in 1971. As luck would have it, that year Washington's birthday, February 22, fell on a Monday. (At the time, Washington's birthday and Lincoln's birthday were observed on two separate days; this changed in 1981 with the establishment of the Martin Luther King, Jr. Day.) Because of how the law was written, with Monday indeed being a weekday, Washington's February 22 birthday was celebrated on the fifteenth—the Monday before.

41. Evacuation

Since San Francisco sits on the Pacific rim, we residents always worry about earthquakes and tsunamis. Well, maybe "worry" isn't the right word. When a tsunami warning was issued in 2011 after a magnitude 8.9 earthquake in Japan, people here flocked to the beach to see. They were disappointed at the measly one-foot waves.

But we're well prepared. All roads at the beach have "Tsunami Evacuation Route" signs, pointing uphill, away from the ocean. As I've overheard one visitor comment, "I don't know what I'd do if there weren't any signs."

I've also noted generic "Evacuation Route" signs in other cities, like Boston, though I don't quite know what they'd be evacuating from. Cape Cod has them too, pointing westward, which feel like a bit of an oxymoron (imagine evacuating Cape Cod!). I've always wondered if, after 9/11, the Department of Homeland Security offered cities money to plan for emergencies and recipients had to find something to show for the funding.

See: Examiner Staff, "Video: People Flock to Ocean Beach San Francisco to Watch for Tsunami," *San Francisco Examiner*, March 11, 2011, https://www.sfexaminer.com/news/video-people-flock-to-ocean-beach-san-francisco-to-watch-for-tsunami/article_aae4377f-89f0-508b-b46b-3974e68e021d.html (accessed December 27, 2022).

Pacific Ocean

42. Forms and More Forms

Medical institutions are supposed to report medication errors. Most are small ones, without any significance to patient health, though some are big. State oversight committees review these reports and ding any medical practices that don't report enough. That's because they know errors happen, and if we clinicians don't report many, it's assumed we're concealing them. I tried to report an error once, which would have made our pharmacist happy, since he had to report to the state. But the form was so long that I gave up on it. Alas.

Home health agencies, whose nurses make house visits for frail people, like patients recently discharged from hospitals, send primary care providers long, detailed assessments, nursing plans, and medical orders as part of their billing protocol. Because they all require our signature, each one begins "Urgent" because the agency can't bill and get paid until we sign. Medicare and Medicaid require copious documentation to prevent fraud.

I feel bad for the nurses, who must spend an inordinate amount of time drafting these. Because the truth is that we providers simply sign and return them without reading a word. If we seriously read and thought about them, we'd never have time to take care of patients. Form fatigue is a real phenomenon.

Years ago, I read in a newspaper that somewhere in Tennessee, residents reported seeing a UFO. A local TV station inquired of the nearby Air Force base. A spokesperson told them, "A few years ago we saw something, and had to fill out so many forms, that we've never seen anything since."

43. Death Certificates

Death certificates are an important source of health information, and lots of government policy and funding depends on knowing why we die. But several experiences have awakened me to the potential underlying flaws of this intelligence gathering.

Case No. 1: A sixty-three-year-old patient of mine was brought to an ER after a car accident, dead on arrival. The funeral home said I needed to complete the death certificate; I said the ER should, since they knew what had happened. The local coroner called me, and in a gruff voice rattled off, "It's not the ER's job, it was a low-speed single-car accident, no signs of trauma," then hung up. Well, the man had severe heart failure (a huge weak heart, which could be prone to abnormal rhythms). So I called it, "sudden cardiac death" (in a sense everyone who dies has "sudden cardiac death"). Whatever.

Case No. 2: A few years ago, I learned that one of my patients had died unexpectedly two months earlier, at age seventy-three. Our nutritionist had heard this from his wife, who relayed that the coroner informed her that it was from "clogged coronary arteries," i.e., a heart attack. That didn't reflect well on me since my job as primary care provider is to prevent such things. The man did have diabetes and high blood pressure, but not only had both conditions been well-controlled, he was also in excellent shape, running five miles a day (he'd played professional sports in his youth). I called the wife.

She described how her husband had developed vomiting and diarrhea for five days and became dehydrated. He sought care at a hospital's urgent care clinic, where they rehydrated him with IV fluids, drew blood tests (which got lost), and discharged him. After his symptoms promptly returned the next morning, she "begged him" to go back again, but he refused. He died that night.

How sad. But it certainly didn't sound like a heart attack. The hospital thought he'd had an intestinal infection, and I surely didn't know all the details, though such symptoms can be due to sepsis (germs in the blood) or a number of terrible diseases. But a heart attack?

The wife then explained how the coroner proceeded once he came out to her house. He looked at my patient's medicines, recognized that some were for diabetes and hypertension, and rapidly concluded "clogged arteries." Coroners, you see, are not inclined to exhaust their budgets on unnecessary autopsies, and only order them when a crime or overdose seem likely. That surely wasn't the case here, so "heart attack" seemed as good (and quick) as anything. Hmmm. At least after hearing what happened, I felt better about my medical management.

Case No. 3: A doctor I work with received a call from a funeral parlor. One of his very elderly patients had died at home, and they needed a death certificate in order to proceed with the funeral. My colleague wrote "possible heart attack." The funeral home said, "no good," so he revised it to "probable heart attack." They still objected, but my colleague refused to write anything more definitive ("How do I know what he died from?"), so the funeral home conceded, and the man was buried.

A few months later, the doctor fielded a call from an angry university researcher who specialized in mortality statistics. "You can't put presumptive causes [i.e., make a guess] on death certificates!" My colleague later confided, "If I hadn't been so busy with patients, I'd have told him, 'Get out of your [expletive] ivory tower and come down to the real world!'"

MORAL—In medicine at least, we have an expression about data and statistics, "GIGO" ("Garbage In, Garbage Out"). Studies show that "heart attacks" are America's number-one cause of death, and you'd agree if you look at death certificates alone. But given my experiences, I'm always a little skeptical of research based on them.

44. Subversive

Museums are free in London. A friend there described how, after a violin lesson, he stopped by the British Museum for a quick look around on his way home but was refused entry. His instrument was prohibited and the cloakroom wouldn't check it for him. Indeed, a sign at the entrance announced, "Adult scooters, skateboards and musical instruments are not allowed onto the premises." He inquired why. The guard at the door explained, "You might begin to play it."

45. The Not-Infallible X-ray

My friend Edward once described how flying home from a small Midwestern airport, he bought a bottle of tax-free liquor. He put it in his carry-on backpack, and then had to pee. The nearest restroom sign pointed down a hallway which happened to lead past the security check-in line, and he realized only too late that he'd be stuck passing back through with the liquor on him.

With no other choice, he put the bottle in the plastic tray to be scanned and placed his backpack on top of it, fully expecting to be caught. The Transportation Security Administration (TSA) agent spotted the obvious culprit on the X-ray, and advised him, "You have a bottle in the backpack." My friend innocently replied, "I don't think so." As the agent lifted the backpack to inspect its contents, Edward whisked the bottle off the tray and behind his back.

Lo and behold, the backpack itself was indeed clean. The TSA fellow seemed puzzled but waved him on. No crime here, and Edward hadn't lied. I'm not sure what educational requirements are stipulated for TSA employment, surely not a degree in common sense.

46. Spending Down in Style

When my mother required permanent nursing home care, we discovered she would have qualified for Medicaid once she spent all her money down to only $2,000 in assets. As power of attorney, though, I couldn't simply give her money away (like, to family). At least, not legally. But an estate lawyer explained that Medicaid doesn't count a car in these assets, presumably so that family could visit her or someone else could bring her whatever supplies she might require. The upside is that the car could be anything—even a Rolls Royce.

Well, I could have bought one as a money shelter, then sold it after her death. But we really didn't want such a target parked on the streets of San Francisco. We settled for a more modest vehicle, which we're still using. It always feels strange to me, the idea of visiting my mom in a nursing home in a Rolls.

Economy:
Money, Money, Money

"He who will not economize will have to agonize."

—Confucius

"Economy is too late at the bottom of the purse."

—Seneca

"Anyone who lives within their means
suffers from a lack of imagination."

—Oscar Wilde

47. Mink Neckties

On a plane to Europe in 1971, I sat next to a man who described his occupation as "designer." He came up with designs for products, sketching them out and marketing them to manufacturers. His latest idea was a mink necktie.

Who'd purchase one of those? As the gentleman explained, it would be geared toward a self-important, conceited snob who wanted the most expensive something in the world but who wasn't rich. The targeted buyer wouldn't be able to afford the world's most expensive car, house, or even wristwatch, but a mink necktie for $200 back then was within his means. Also, it was conducive to showing off wherever and whenever.

I tried searching on "mink necktie" recently, but all results referred to the color mink. I'm not sure how my airplane acquaintance made out. Maybe he scored a few hits and went on to the next lucrative idea for quick cash.

48. Mad Cow Disease: Knackers, Greaves, Downers, and More

"Mad Cow" disease causes progressive brain damage with psychiatric symptoms, behavioral changes, movement abnormalities, and memory disturbances, leading to death within a year. Technically called bovine spongiform encephalopathy, it's transmitted by eating beef contaminated with a prion—not a germ, but an abnormal protein, which withstands heat and thus can't be destroyed. These prions originated in sheep, causing a disease scrapie, and there are lots of sheep in Britain, where Mad Cow began (the first human case was identified in 1996). One plausible theory for its origin and spread among cattle there in the 1980s was the process of rendering.

In Britain, there are (or were) informal self-employed workers called "knackers," who pick up roadkill and other dead animals in the countryside, then "render" them by boiling them down in backyard furnaces, skimming their fat from the top and selling it to chemical firms. The leftover dregs, called "greaves," were often mixed into animal food. That's where the prions were; cows ate them, and people ate the cows, with all this nasty stuff from sheep brains unknowingly hidden in the meat.

Such recyclers have existed throughout the ages, at least in Europe. We don't really have knackers in America, so we've been pretty much spared the horrors of Mad Cow. There is some risk from "downer" cows (those too weak to walk to the slaughterhouse), which get killed on the spot. Their meat winds up in pet and animal food. But the US has been vigilant about scrapie, so it's rarely seen here.

If you can stomach it, here's a marvelously gross article on rendering: Sandra Blakeslee, "Fear of Disease Prompts New Look at Rendering," *New York Times*, March 11, 1997, https://www.nytimes.com/1997/03/11/science/fear-of-disease-prompts-new-look-at-rendering.html (accessed December 27, 2022).

On the disease in general: CNN Editorial Research, "Mad Cow Disease Fast Facts," *CNN Health*, May 30, 2022, https://www.cnn.com/2013/07/02/health/mad-cow-disease-fast-facts/index.html (accessed February 11, 2023).

49. What's a Street Really Worth?

Presidio Terrace is a small private street in San Francisco where over thirty extremely wealthy families live in mansions. It has a single, guarded access point, and features attractive islands with trees and gorgeous gardens. The late senator Diane Feinstein was a former resident, and the UK Consul General a more recent one. But in 2015, the city's Tax Collector put the street itself up for auction, since almost $1,000 in delinquent taxes, plus interest and penalties, had accrued for over thirty years on its $14 annual property tax fee. Apparently, the bills had been sent to a defunct address of the homeowner association's old accountant and were never paid. A husband-and-wife real estate agency bid and bought the street for $90,000, hoping to profit from charging for the street's 120 available parking spaces, or perhaps selling it all forward.

Property owners were shocked at the turn of events, to say the least. They objected to not having received fair warning about the auction. A spokeswoman for the tax office replied, with little sympathy, "Ninety-nine percent of property owners in San Francisco know what they need to do, and they pay their taxes on time—and they keep their mailing address up to date."

The San Francisco Board of Supervisors voted seven to four to rescind the sale. The supervisors offered various rationales for their decision, such as the lack of due process and semantic differences as to whether the street was a "vacant" or "occupied" property. Local newspaper readers were in general indignant, though surely not surprised, that politicians sided with the homeowners. At least they got their laughs watching the rich squirm for a while.

See: Phillip Matier and Andrew Ross, "Rich SF residents Get a Shock: Someone Bought Their Street," *San Francisco Chronicle*, August 7, 2017 / updated August 9, 2017, https://www.sfchronicle.com/bayarea/matier-ross/article/Rich-SF-residents-get-a-shock-Someone-bought-11738236.php (accessed December 27, 2022).

Adam Brinklow, "Presidio Terrace: Supervisors Explain Why They Overturned Sale of Private Street," *Curbed San Francisco*, December 1, 2017, https://sf.curbed.com/2017/12/1/16721714/presidio-terrace-supervisors-ex-plain-rich-wealthy-street (accessed December 24, 2022).

50. One "Brilliant" Crime, and a Gem of Another

a) Stop on a Dime

One night in Philadelphia in 2023, a gang of thieves broke into a US Mint truck loaded with $750,000 ready for transport and made off with almost a third of the contents—all in dimes. The approximately two million coins weighed about five tons. What puzzled police the most is how the crooks expected to spend the loot. Haul it into an electronics store? Buy a car??? Maybe North Korea or Al-Qaeda would find a way to make use.

The heist otherwise seemed well planned: the truck driver had parked in a Walmart lot and slept elsewhere for the night, which is not unusual in the industry. The thieves had plenty of time to move five tons of the small metal disks. Philadelphia cops later spent hours scooping up the thousands of coins which got left scattered on the pavement. One officer advised people with full piggy banks at home, "This is probably not the time to cash them in."

See: Eduardo Medina, "Thieves Break into Vehicle and Make Off with $200,000 … in Dimes," *New York Times*, April 14, 2023, https://www.nytimes.com/2023/04/14/us/philadelphia-dimes-stolen-truck.html (accessed April 17, 2023).

b) Stuck on a Stick

In 1963, thieves neatly hijacked a station wagon transporting three million dollars' worth of jewels between a company's New York City offices. Well, almost. Most of the crooks whisked the few employees away in a stolen vehicle, while another was assigned to drive off with the loot in the company's car. But the station wagon was a stick shift, and he didn't know how to use it. After jerking and stalling a number of times, he gave up and walked away emptyhanded.

Nearby, some construction workers were puzzled by the strange goings-on, so they went over to explore. And helped themselves to the gems. They also helped themselves to a bit too much liquor at a weekend party and bragged about the gems a bit too much. Another guest squealed to the cops. A core group of workers denied everything until police questioned them separately, when they then pointed fingers at each other. In the end, perhaps everyone who'd scooped up any jewels turned them in; nobody ever heard from the original thieves.

The jewelry company recouped its wares. It refined its practices, establishhing more precautions, but continued to drive inventory between offices. What dismayed its employees the most was that all the new vehicles were fully automatic.

Google the title below to read a hilarious 10-page magazine account.

See: Paul Mandel, "The Gigantic Gem Goof," *Life*, February 7, 1964, https://books.google.com/books?id=GFQEAAAAMBAJ&pg=PA84&lp-g=PA84&dq=jewel+truck+robbery+new+york+stick+shift+construc-tion+work&source=bl&ots=sNOmA3lIP3&sig=ACfU3U1HWyGx2Ml-II3k1d7MnKX6To45upA&hl=en&sa=X&ved=2ahUKEwio59DK_rH-AhWmn-GoFHX47AEMQ6AF6BAg2EAM#v=onepage&q&f=false (accessed April17, 2023).

51. Pack Them In, Help Them Out

The Barnum & Bailey Circus was once immensely popular. Visitors often spent their entire day at the event, crimping profit margins. At such moments, P.T. Barnum would put up a sign that read, "This Way to the Egress." People would flock down a corridor to explore, expecting a weird bird or something, then pass through a door, and find themselves on the street. "Egress," after all, simply means "exit." The opposite is Ingress, but to get back into the circus, patrons would have to pay again.

See: "Welcome to the Egress!" *P.T. Barnum*, http://www.ptbarnum.org/egress. html (accessed December 24, 2022).

52. Everybody Pays in San Francisco

He should have stuck with reindeer on rooftops.

53. Advertisers Ought to Be Wiser

Over the years, I've occasionally profited from not-so-smart advertising ploys. For example, in the early 1990s, when people still used road maps, I received an unsolicited postcard from a life insurance company offering one of those big *Rand McNally* road atlases for free if I would simply send them my name, phone number, and birthday. Never one to turn down anything free, I complied. But since I really didn't want a callback, for my "birthday," I wrote the year as 1898. I didn't think anybody would be too interested in selling me life insurance.

I got my road atlas and forgot about it. Several months later, though, I received a call: "Is this Steven Leiner?" "Yes," I replied reflexively. It was the life insurance people! I quickly turned my mouth to the side and shouted, "Grandpa, Grandpa—it's for you."

They hung up!

Before cell phones, we had "calling cards" for when you were away. At a pay phone booth, you punched in or read out a PIN to pay for the call without having to carry around a ton of change. Well, thieves had clever ways to steal the PINs in public places, either by eavesdropping or spying on phone keypads from afar with binoculars.

In 1993, we flew to New York for a family emergency. We left in a disorganized rush, and while away, I discovered my AT&T card no longer worked. Apparently, someone had pilfered the PIN at the San Francisco airport and passed it on (sold it) to two others, who quickly became four, and on and on. In under an hour, dozens of people had totaled $2,000 worth of international calls. AT&T's fraud checkers promptly cancelled the card.

The AT&T rep was very nice. Not only did she tell me I wouldn't be responsible for the charges, but she also offered to send me the phone numbers of the thieves and accomplices, a gesture that I quickly declined. I never got billed, and that was that.

But even though I had an AT&T card, my landline carrier was Sprint. Several months later, I received an unsolicited offer from AT&T: if I changed carriers, they'd send me $75. So, I did just that, cashed the check ... and then promptly switched back to Sprint. Several months later a similar offer arrived, and I restarted the whole process. I must have made over $300 off AT&T before the offers finally stopped coming.

My guess is that because of the stolen calling card, their system tagged me as a big spender, so they tried to snag me as a permanent customer. I've always wondered if anyone lost their job over that dumb attempt.

54. Fighting the Bill

Janice, a poor college graduate I knew here in San Francisco, described how she had lost her health insurance but, fortunately, qualified for Medicaid. She asked her long-time doctor's office if they accepted it; the staff said yes, so she attended her scheduled appointment. A few months later she received a $200 bill, since it turned out they didn't accept Medicaid patients after all (a common policy in many private practices because reimbursement is low). She complained, but to no avail.

I told Janice to demand to speak to the supervisor. The office manager agreed to decrease the amount to $100. It was still a lot for her, but she felt resigned that she'd never be able to get it any lower.

I suggested she tell the office manager that she'd pay the $100 but could only afford five dollars per month. She did, and the office manager gave up—organizing and processing these payments would likely cost more in staff time than the amount owed. They cancelled the bill completely. I bought Janice a drink to celebrate.

On the topic of unfair billing: I had my own edifying run-in with AT&T, who sold me a special travel plan for a trip to Europe and then billed me $89 in extra long-distance fees that they hadn't explained (or had explained wrong). I was a longtime AT&T customer, and the amount should have been trivial to them, but the first-tier telephone rep I spoke to didn't have the power to waive anything. I asked for the supervisor, who also refused to cancel the amount. That surprised me, and pissed me off, so I asked, "Do you know the phone number for Comcast?" She immediately responded, "Let me connect you with our Loyalty Specialist." Loyalty Specialist? You don't say! I'd never heard of that position before, but that lady was high enough up to quickly erase the charge.

The next time you're fighting a bill, ask for the supervisor at the first sign of being stonewalled. If the supervisor won't bend, ask for the "Loyalty Specialist." It's apparently a standard position in businesses, though not something that's disclosed to consumers.

55. Brushing Teeth

I once happened to observe a friend brushing her teeth and was shocked at the sight of her squeezing a copious amount of toothpaste onto her brush. I asked her why she used so much, since a mere smidgeon lathers up my mouth quite well. She couldn't answer; she had simply always done so, she explained. My guess is that this is how she saw it done on a TV ad, maybe as a kid, and the habit stuck. She must have bought a lot more tubes than I have over the years. Which, I'm guessing, is the point of all those advertisements.

I admit to having a strange curiosity about commercials, the more unrealistic (and misleading) the better. Take the automobile commercials showing a car zoom in the air from one bridge to another, only for a pop-up or Very Serious Voice to appear warning viewers not to attempt the stunt. Company lawyers are certainly cautious. We don't watch TV much, so we only have a small modest screen. I complain to my wife about wanting a bigger one, just so I can read the fine print on the advertisements.

56. No to Pickleball
(Maybe)

I n summer of 2023, a San Francisco homeowner began a petition
to close a pickleball court at a nearby playground. According
to the *San Francisco Chronicle*, the lady was not only distressed by
the constant "grating" noise of ball-on-paddle but also argued that
it affected wildlife and the "fragile ecosystem." She and another
neighbor demanded that play be suspended pending an environ-
mental study. The petition read, "This isn't just about us—it's about
preserving nature for future generations."

Another complaint mentioned therein was how the noise
depressed local property values. The playground happened to sit in
a particularly ritzy neighborhood. The petitioner's eight-bedroom
house was listed on the local market for $36 million ... and included
its own private outdoor pickleball court.

The director of the city's recreation and park department noted,
"Not everyone can afford a pickleball court in their backyard. That's
why it's nice to have them in public parks." A member of a pickleball
advocacy group commented, "We were just rolling on the floor."

See: J.K. Dineen, "'Hypocrisy of Rich': S.F. Woman Trying to Shut Down
Pickleball Court Has One in Her Backyard," *San Francisco Chronicle*, August
30, 2023, https://www.sfchronicle.com/sf/article/pickleball-court-presi-
dio-heights-18336716.php (accessed September 3, 2023).

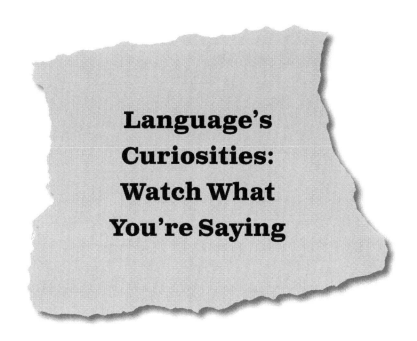

Language's Curiosities: Watch What You're Saying

"The language of Friendship is not words but meanings."
—Henry David Thoreau, *A Week on the Concord and Merrimack Rivers*

"Language is the origin of misunderstandings."
—Antoine de Saint-Exupéry, *The Little Prince*

"The misuse of language induces evil in the soul."
—Socrates

57. Gender Neutrals

Most jobs now employ gender-neutral terms in place of older terminology. For example, "fireman" is now "firefighter"; "mailman" now "mail carrier"; "stewardess" now "flight attendant"; "waiter/waitress" now "server"; "actor/actress" now simply "actor"; etc.

However, there remain some words we only use in the masculine. These include "henchman," "strongman," "conman," "hitman." Maybe they still tend to be men? Shouldn't be. We may need to adopt new terms such as "henchpeople," "hitpeople."

58. Artfully Put

An attorney friend attended a lecture for lawyers about defamation lawsuits. One speaker suggested how to phrase a reference letter for a lazy employee seeking a new job: "You're lucky to get them to work for you."

No defamation there.

59. If Zuckerberg Only Knew

In 2021, Facebook's Mark Zuckerberg announced to great fanfare the rebranding of the company to "Meta," standing for the Metaverse—a virtual world where people simulate "reality." But for many years already, "meta" has been a common abbreviation in the transgender community for "metoidioplasty," the surgical procedure of enlarging the clitoris to create a penis for transgender female-to-males. Less invasive than the larger "phalloplasty," or "neo-penis," the "meta" also retains clitoral sensation and can achieve orgasm.

Hopefully the transgender community will feel complimented by Mr. Zuckerberg's coopting of their term. And hopefully Facebook will feel equally proud.

See: deadaccount22, "The Surgery," *Accidentally Gay*, February 19, 2017, https://accidentallygay.com/2017/02/19/the-surgery/ (accessed April 25, 2023).

60. Going to the Bathroom

When I first traveled abroad in 1972, I asked a friend in Sweden I was staying with, "Where's the bathroom?" "What for?" she replied. In Europe, now as well as then, the bathroom is where you take a bath in a tub or wash your hands in the sink. To pee, you seek out a "toilet," a separate room that contains a toilet, often with a sink but maybe not.

I worked in rural Appalachia in the early 1980s, when perhaps half of the houses lacked indoor plumbing. The expression there was, "I have to go out," referring to the outhouse. When a mother brought her baby with diarrhea to my emergency room, she might have described how the child in diapers "goes out" over and over. If tempted to laugh at that, at least reflect how we ourselves might well say the kid keeps "going to the bathroom."

61. Foreign Language Problems

A nurse I knew from Montreal, Quebec, who spoke fluent, if not perfect, English (French was her first language), once helped care for a teenage girl who'd been brought to the emergency room for head trauma with mild concussion. When the girl's parents arrived a little later, my friend tried to reassure them that she was okay, saying, "Don't worry, she was just a little knocked up." The parents got agitated, she still tried to reassure them, same way. Parents got even more upset. Finally, the mom asked, "Do you mean knocked out?" "Right, same thing," reassured my friend. "NOT the same thing!"

A Swedish woman described how she had spent a year in a Minnesota high school as an exchange student. Her classmates there would often ask her, "What was the first word you learned in English?" To which my friend would innocently reply: "cock." It was from a simple elementary school barnyard story. She was constantly taken aback by two things: a) her American classmates' reactions; and b) the fact that nobody ever explained their reaction. It took a while before she finally found out.

62. More on Foreign Languages

You'd think advertisers would be bright enough to make sure their target audiences knew what they were trying to sell them. But around San Francisco, I frequently see billboard advertisements for major brand names written in quite unintelligible Spanish. Most likely the companies have some bilingual staff person translate the original ad from English (or use Google). The non-professional wants to be exact, so they translate word-for-word (as opposed to idiomatically), which is never the way anybody speaks. Latinos I know say they usually can't understand the signs, which must have cost a fair bit to create. I always laugh when I see them.

Even trained interpreters can miss subtleties. I've had at least three patients who had received brief courses of opioid pain medicine for fractures or surgery, and, since narcotics may constipate, also got a concurrent prescription for stool-softeners (dioctyl succinate, Colace®, etc.). The interpreters typically translated the reasoning as "*para constipación.*" But in several Central American countries, "*constipación*" means "nasal congestion" (for the English word "constipated," people may say "*estítico*" or "*estreñido*"). So these puzzled patients would ask me what the little red, oil-containing capsules are for, holding them confusedly in front of their noses and mouths wondering, "Where does it go?"

Speaking of mixed-up Spanish translations, there's a popular old myth that Chevrolet's 1962 revolutionary compact, the Chevy Nova, did poorly in Latin America because in Spanish "*no va*" means "doesn't go." It wasn't true, however; the car sold just fine.

McDonald's was said to have almost translated its "Big Mac" into French as "Le Mac Gros," but reversed course when they learned that *le maquereau* (pronounced virtually the·same) literally means "mackerel," slang for "pimp."

See: David Mikkelson, "Did the Chevrolet Nova Fail to Sell in Spanish-Speaking Countries?" *Snopes*, April 2, 1999, https://www.snopes.com/fact-check/chevrolet-nova-name-spanish/ (accessed December 26, 2022).

63. Foreign Languages, Even More

Two doctors from Taiwan's Center for Disease Control visited our San Francisco HIV Clinic, and after two hours of program sharing (they spoke excellent English), we all posed for a picture. Someone on our staff exclaimed, "Say 'cheese.'" I asked our guests what people say in Chinese for photos, and one of them replied, "Cheese."

In English there's a common expression, "It's all Greek to me." Other languages use it also. But what do they say in Greece? "It's all Chinese to me."

I speak fairly fluent Spanish, and out of curiosity, ask native speakers how they communicate various English idioms. For example, to shrug something off as trivial or meaningless, we might say, "That's like spitting in the ocean." The Spanish equivalent is, "Like pulling one hair off a cat." We say, "Don't hold your breath;" they say "Wait a while, but better lying down." For our "Once in a blue moon," in Central America it's "When the bishop stops by." (Bishops proudly boasted of visiting remote villages in their rural dioceses, though in practice rarely made the trip.)

During World War II, lest anybody inadvertently divulge information of potential interest to spies, a widespread mantra warned, "Loose lips sink ships." Another expression was "Walls have ears." During El Salvador's civil war, the pro-guerrilla civilian support base would exhort, "If your mouth stays shut, flies can't get in."

For a hilarious "global idioms quiz" from Britain's *The Guardian*, search "Guardian Wheel Spinning Hamster Dead" (based on a new book).

64. Thumbs Up!
(Thumbs Down?)

L ots of people use the thumbs-up emoji to indicate "like" or "agree," but few know where it originated. In ancient Rome, gladiators fought to the death while spectators cheered. If one fighter disarmed and pinned his opponent on the ground, sword to throat, the victor would turn to the emperor in the stands. If the emperor gave a "thumbs up," it meant the victor could take the win but spare the life (ostensibly because the loser fought well). But a "thumbs down" from the almighty ... well, you can imagine what happened. Something to think about the next time you use an emoji for texting "no" to your mom.

Other terms Generation Z may use without understanding:

"CC" in an email means "carbon copy." Before computers, typists used carbon paper to make copies of their work. You placed a piece of carbon paper—a filmy page with carbon on the underside—between the "original" page you were typing and the page you wanted as a copy. Typing on the original, the smudgy carbon would reproduce the strokes onto the second page, the "carbon copy." When I showed one to my teenage daughters years ago, they marveled at how pretty it looked (though, it should be mentioned, they didn't see how smudgy the process could be).

"Cut and paste": we literally did this to write school papers. For the many of us who couldn't type fluently, we'd initially write in longhand, editing over and over before daring to type up a final copy. To move sentences and paragraphs around in our rough drafts, we'd literally cut and paste (or tape or staple) them where we wanted.

My five-year-old daughter once played a line for her violin teacher somewhat sloppily. When her teacher asked, "What did you think of that?" Leah replied, "It sucked." The teacher gasped, wide-eyed, at the seemingly shocking response from a little girl.

More recently, out of curiosity, I've asked a number of coworkers who are Leah's age (she's now in her twenties) if they know where the expression comes from; they haven't. After all, we use it quite indiscriminately and in a completely innocuous way. But it originated from a vile homophobic slur. Telling someone they "suck" once referred to a certain sexual act. It was considered the epitome of an insult.

And then there's "snafu," often used for bureaucratic impasses. Again, we say it casually. But it originated from World War II army slang, as an acronym for "Situation Normal, All F'ed Up." When I was young, my father explained how the phrase meant "All Fouled Up;" I figured it out as I got older.

65. Catching Spies

There are lots of good stories about seemingly miniscule details Allied spies got wrong during World War II, leading to their detection. Here are some of the best examples:

Counting on fingers: Most Americans count from their index finger (one) to their pinky (four), then use their thumb to mean "five." Europeans begin with the thumb (one) and then proceed toward the pinky.

Americans anchor their meat with the fork in their left hand, cut with the knife in the right, then "politely" transfer the fork to the right hand to eat. Europeans simply eat with the fork still in the left.

Buttons in some countries are sewn in parallel stitches, and in others in cross stitches. For spy and fashion buffs, see below for an article about all the subtleties of clothing that WWII British spies and their agencies dealt with.

See: Jocely Sears, "Clothing Britain's Spies During World War II," *JStor Daily*, August 8, 2018, https://daily.jstor.org/clothing-britains-spies-wwii/ (accessed December 24, 2022).

66. How Cold Is It?

In winter 1972, we were happily chatting away, riding in a packed van above the Arctic Circle. I was in my mid-twenties, most of my accompanying Swedish friends there were a bit younger, while Ricky, an American exchange student, was a high school senior. He was shy and usually quiet, not knowing much Swedish. But during a pause in the conversation, he piped up with a question in English, "Marina, what did you say that word was?"

Marina chuckled and replied, "Knullande" (nu-LAN-de), which literally means "fucking." Ricky struggled to utter his phrase, "Det är knullande kallt ute," translating word for word, "It's fucking cold outside."

Nobody understood. I cracked up, knowing what he meant, and Marina laughed too.

Ricky asked mournfully, "You don't say that?"

She suggested, "Something might be knullande hot, but certainly not knullande cold."

If you really wanted to express the same sentiment in Swedish, you'd use what's considered a nasty profanity: "jävligt" (YAEV-ligt), meaning "damn." It comes from the word "djävel," meaning "devil." That doesn't quite cut it in English. If a visiting Swede were to tell us it's "devilishly" cold out, we either wouldn't understand or would just think it sounded stupid.

Swear words in Swedish tend to have religious derivations, even if few people there today are at all observant. Cultures traditionally use their taboos to curse. In English, ours are sexual. Indeed, it often seems to me that sex is our new religion.

For example, Catholic hospitals will claim freedom of religion when denying contraceptive or abortion services. In the 1950s, the Catholic Church's concern was to forbid its flock from visiting other religions' churches and temples. I doubt that a baker or website designer who objects to crafting gay marriage themes would mind assisting nonbelievers like Jews, Muslims, or Hindus, though they're ostensibly heading down the road to hell.

English's taboos used to include religious terms. I once took my teenage daughter and her friend to Gilbert and Sullivan's operetta *HMS Pinafore*, written in 1878. In Act 1, the captain touts how polite he is, singing, "I never use a big, big D-." The girls turned to me and whispered, "What's that?" "Damn," I explained. They raised their eyebrows and shook their heads, as if to say "How dumb."

Unless you're a native speaker, never swear in a foreign language, no matter how fluent you may be. Your accent and intonation will sound just the least bit off, which will make the profanity more disturbing than you may have imagined. Unless, of course, you intended to truly offend. In which case, be prepared for retaliation.

67. Prayer in the Sky

For over thirty years, from the 1970s to 2012, Alaska Airlines not only served free food to passengers but included a prayer card on the tray. The latter, bearing various quotes from the Book of Psalms, were meant to facilitate saying grace for the meal, though nobody knew that (from 2006 on, it was only available in first-class). Eventually complaints outnumbered praises, and the company dropped the practice.

Prayer cards for airplane passengers? There's an old saying, "There are no atheists in foxholes" (i.e. everyone believes in God when the shells come soaring overhead). Is that analogous for those who choose to fly Alaska?

See: Mark Memmot, "Alaska Airlines to Stop Handing Out Prayer Cards," *NPR*, January 25, 2012, https://www.npr.org/sections/the-two-way/2012/01/25/145856318/alaska-airlines-to-stop-handing-out-prayer-cards (accessed December 25, 2022).

68. *Discamus Latine* (Let's Learn Latin)

I was chatting with a young woman from Austria who had recently finished high school. We were speaking English, since I don't know German. We Americans are always impressed how Europeans can be so fluent in English. They study it from early elementary school and immerse themselves in American films and music. But they don't necessarily learn other languages any better than we do.

I asked my new acquaintance if she spoke anything else. She shook her head and mentioned how she had learned a little Latin in school. Latin? I didn't think that schools anywhere still taught it, though apparently in Europe they do. It was once the world's lingua franca, but nobody has diplomatic relationships with ancient Rome these days. I'd be hard pressed to imagine how anybody might ever use it. She explained that she had the option of either Latin or French, and she regretted her choice.

Yet in 1973 a Greek man told me how he had met a fellow from Hungary who didn't speak English. Neither of the two spoke each other's language. But back then, they had both learned Latin in school and were able to converse in it. I was impressed—like traveling back in time by millennia.

69. Janus Words

Also called contranyms, antagonyms, or auto-antonyms, these are words with two completely opposite meanings. Like "fast": as in "he ran fast" (= moving rapidly), and "the dye remained fast" (= fixed, unchanging). Janus was the Roman god with two faces, each looking in opposite directions (January, which looks backward to the old year and forward to the new one, was named for him).

Here's a sample of my collection of Janus words and phrases:

i)   heeding, obeying;   MINDING
     objecting

He minded when I told him to mind what I said to do.

ii) prevents errors;   OVERSIGHT
     causes errors

There were lots of oversights due to lack of oversight.

iii) what successful explorers do,   STRIKE OUT
         on an expedition;
     what failed explorers do

On day one, they were stoked as they struck out on their exciting expedition. At the end, they struck out, finding nothing.

iv) to approve;   SANCTION
     a prohibition

Congress sanctioned the Iran sanctions.

v)   the direction things go   DOWNHILL
        when sailing's smooth;
     the direction things go when all falls apart

The CEO predicted, "We're over the hard part: it's all downhill from here." But things crashed, and the company went
downhill.

vi) to complete a missing assignment;   MAKE UP
     to fake a missing assignment

The teacher let me make up the late report, then claimed I
made it up and failed me.

vii) to establish and consolidate an agreement;   FORGE
     to fake or falsify an agreement

The enemies forged an agreement. An underling claimed to
leak the document, which turned out to be forged.

viii) a flight that is uncertain to depart;   UP IN THE AIR
      a flight that is on its way

My vacation plans to Europe were up in the air; with the
weather so iffy, the flight was likely to be cancelled. But it took
off, and right now I'm up in the air over the Atlantic.

ix) most severe;   FIRST-DEGREE
     least severe

When the victim died of third-degree burns, the assailant was
charged with first-degree murder.

x) diminish someone's reputation;   DEMEAN
    behave so as to maintain someone's reputation

(explanation: a lawyer explained how in his state, all new
attorneys took an oath "to demean the profession," an archaic
meaning from the word "demeanor")

The new lawyer swore to always "demean the profession." He
later demeaned it when he joined the mob.

xi) to sprinkle powder on;   DUST
     to clean powder off

He dusted powder all over the bathroom, so now I must dust
the washbasin ornaments.

xii) to lock the barn;   BOLT
      to escape from the barn

The farmer thought he had bolted the barn door, but the bull
bolted out easily.

xiii) a sick patient who's now all better   CURED
      after treatment,
   a dead patient who lies embalmed in an open casket

After Roberta was cured of her illness, she went to her neighbor Bill's funeral, where he lay elegantly in casket, cured stiff from head to toe.

xiv) to invite someone to whom you're   TAKE OUT
      attracted on a date;
   to kill someone

The hitman took the victim out on a date in his car, drove to an isolated area and took her out.

xv) having a feeling of boredom, dullness,   IN (A) RUT
      with no interest in anything;

    participating in highly energetic mating
     rituals (if you're a male ruminant)

(explanation: "in rut" is a biological term for the deer stag's state during breeding season, when the female doe is in heat)

No example here—I guess I've never thought "I'm in a rut," nor "in rut" before sex (I'm not a stag).

COVID:
Panning the
Pandemic

"A plague on both your houses!"

—William Shakespeare, *Romeo and Juliet*

"Festivals cause diseases, since they
lighten cares but increase gluttony."

—Apollonius of Tyana

"The plague ... is merely Nature's fortuitous mani-
festation of her purposeless objectionableness."

—Ambrose Bierce, *The Devil's Dictionary*

70. The CDC Opines on COVID and Pets

In 2020, at the beginning of the pandemic, the US Centers for Disease Control and Prevention (CDC) advised pet owners to keep their dogs and cats six feet apart, since it was theoretically possible for them to harbor and spread the COVID virus. At the time, a friend lamented to me how devastated her outdoor cat would be to hear this. Fortunately for my friend's cat, this "recommendation" can no longer be found on their website—the CDC was receiving enough embarrassing press at the time to open themselves up for more.

71. Jumping the Line for COVID Vaccines

In February of 2021, two apparent gray-haired grannies in Florida, wearing bonnets and gloves, showed up at a health center to receive COVID vaccines. At the time, the brand-new shots were still restricted by age groups, with the elderly—at highest risk—going first. The women had scored their first doses and vaccination cards without any issue. But when they showed up for their second doses, it was discovered that these "grandmothers" were actually thirty-four and forty-four years old. They were turned over to the police, who could only cite them for trespassing. The incident was considered scandalous enough that it even made the news in the UK.

In a similar, though more inspiring, case of vaccine-related mistaken identity, around the same time a thirty-two-year-old man in Liverpool, England, found himself offered an unsolicited appointment for the COVID vaccine. At that time in the UK, it was limited to persons over fifty or those with underlying medical conditions. It seemed like he did have such a condition; as far as the authorities were concerned, he was morbidly obese, even extremely so. At a recent appointment with his regular doctor, his height measured six feet, two inches but got mistakenly recorded as 6.2 cm (less than three inches). His body mass index (BMI), a common calculation of weight-for-height, came out to 28,000 (a normal BMI is less than twenty-five; morbidly obese is over forty).

The gentleman declined the opportunity, considering it unfair. Health authorities complimented him for his decision, though the man was a bit concerned that nobody seemed alarmed at the risks being so enormously wide, just that he had mistakenly been offered the shot.

See: Kevin Rawlinson, "Florida Women Wear 'Granny' Disguise to Try to Get Covid Vaccine," *Guardian*, February 19, 2021, https://www.theguardian.com/world/2021/feb/19/florida-women-wear-granny-disguise-covid-vaccine (accessed December 27, 2022).

"Covid: Man Offered Vaccine After Error Lists Him as 6.2 cm Tall." *BBC News*, February 18, 2021, https://www.bbc.com/news/uk-england-merseyside-56111209 (accessed December 24, 2022).

72. I Love Flying, Nowhere

In 2020, at the early height of the COVID pandemic, as airlines around the world virtually shut down, many people still longed for the travel experience. So when they were offered an opportunity to fly, thousands of people in Brunei, Taiwan, Japan, and Australia seized the chance. The planes took off, flew around for however long, and landed back where they started. Some airlines called these "scenic flights"; others called them "flights to nowhere."

Passengers were thrilled. One said, "All I want is to be in a window seat and see clouds go by." Others enjoyed the experience of dragging baggage at the airport to check in. Prices ranged from $500 to $3,000, and flights sold out quickly.

Environmentalists were quite critical, to say the least.

See: Tariro Mzezewa, "The Flight Goes Nowhere. And It's Sold Out," *New York Times*, September 19, 2020, https://www.nytimes.com/2020/09/19/travel/airlines-pandemic-flights-to-nowhere.html (accessed December 27, 2022).

73. Morbid Thoughts

At the beginning of the pandemic in March 2020, our future seemed most unsure. At seventy-two years old and being overweight, I was at higher risk of serious illness from COVID-19. Even though I wore my N95 mask faithfully, my medical clinic wasn't the safest place to hang out.

So I decided to write my memoir. I'd had lots of experiences in life, which I wanted my children to know about. My own parents, who'd come from the Silent Generation, never talked about theirs; that's always saddened me, especially since they met while serving in the army in Europe during World War II. I know virtually nothing about what they saw or did. They wanted to protect my sister and me from sad stories, which they tried hard not to recall.

However, I never told my kids what or why I was writing. It seemed a little too morbid. "Just in case I die suddenly, I thought I'd tell you about …" I wrote as quickly as I could, though I kept coming up with more and more things to say.

Then, in early 2021, vaccines became available. I got ongoing booster shots, as it became clear that the only people who were hospitalized or died by that time were the unvaccinated. Doom seemed less and less imminent, and I still had more stories to include.

In early 2023 I told my daughter Leah about my writing and how I hadn't wanted to say anything at first, lest the idea feel too upsetting. She replied, "Dad, in 2020 I was thinking the same thing but was afraid to ask you to write it."

It's nice to know when your children think the same way you do.

74. Vaccine Hesitancy

Here in San Francisco, although most of my patients have been fully vaccinated against COVID, some still refuse. One woman explained her reasoning: she didn't like the idea of putting foreign stuff in her body. Her logic can be debated, but she also smoked cigarettes. I opted not to make this connection for her.

A medical student I knew described how one day, a patient of hers had refused the vaccine. He subscribed to some conspiracy theories, though I don't know which ones. She reported the problem to her supervising physician. After the student returned to the exam room, her supervisor entered with a smile, heard the patient out, and commented, "Did you know there's good evidence that all those ideas are a Russian and Chinese plot to dissuade Americans from getting the vaccine?" The patient scheduled a vaccine appointment then and there.

75. Anti-Vaxxer Takes Up Arms

In December of 2021, an anti-vaxxer in Italy wanted a COVID passport. His solution? Wearing a fake silicone arm covering for his shoulder, when it came time to get his shot. A health worker caught on and reported him; as of press time, he faced judicial charges for the stunt.

See: Angela Giuffrida, "Italian Man Tries to Dodge Covid Vaccine Wearing Fake Arm," *Guardian*, December 3, 2021, https://www.theguardian.com/world/2021/dec/03/italian-man-tries-to-dodge-covid-vaccine-wearing-fake-arm (accessed December 27, 2022).

76. Hiding behind Facemasks

In spring and early summer of 2020, when hospitals were overflowing with COVID-19 patients and supplies of personal protective equipment (PPE) like facemasks were officially designated as scarce, a new vendor appeared offering unlimited inventories. The Face Mask Center advertised FDA-approved N95 respirators to hospitals, nursing homes, and fire departments, both in the United States and globally. Unfortunately (or perhaps fortunately), that same August, the Department of Justice announced that it had busted the operation, which was a ruse run by the Islamic State (ISIS).

Perhaps ISIS schemed to sicken Western health workers with the fake PPE. More likely, it merely sought a quick buck. The DOJ simultaneously interrupted Bitcoin operations by Al-Qaeda and other international terrorist groups.

See: Office of Public Affairs, "Global Disruption of Three Terror Finance Cyber-Enabled Campaigns," *US Department of Justice*, August 13, 2020, https://www.justice.gov/opa/pr/global-disruption-three-terror-finance-cyber-enabled-campaigns (accessed August 26, 2023).

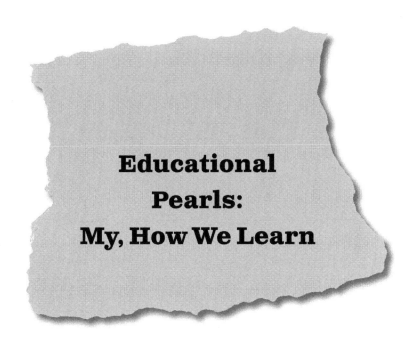

Educational Pearls: My, How We Learn

"In the first place God made idiots. This was for practice. Then He made School Boards."

—Mark Twain, *Following the Equator*

"Education is an admirable thing, but it is well to remember from time to time that nothing that is worth knowing can be taught."

—Oscar Wilde, *Intentions*

"It is always in season for old men to learn."

—Aeschylus, *Agamemnon*

77. Term Papers

My friend Andrea recently described how, in the 1960s, she submitted a lengthy term paper at the end of her senior year high school English class. She didn't recall her grade, only that her teacher returned it without a single note or correction. All he wrote was a comment at the very end, "Too repetitious. Good at times, but you repeat yourself."

Andrea considered that a badge of honor (although I don't think she had it framed).

78. Taking Tests

It was my freshman year at the University of Chicago in 1965, and my girlfriend Denise was failing all her physics tests. She hated the subject. The only reason she took it was because her father insisted she study pre-med. He was an East Coast university professor and thus "knew what was best" for her; he also once said that his wife needed a psychiatrist, but he couldn't afford one. Denise would tremble whenever receiving a letter from him.

This was obviously insane to me—I'll refrain from divulging what I thought of him—but I felt for Denise. I also noticed how she was averaging 20 percent on her one-out-of-four multiple choice tests, which is worse than blind guessing. This was because her physics prof asked tricky questions, and she consistently fell for the pitfalls. One day I suggested she try to figure out the right answer then randomly pick any of the other three choices. Her score rose close to 40 percent.

This strategy might not have been great for her self-esteem, but I wasn't in tune with those sorts of things back then. And, anyway, she didn't care. We broke up after our first year, but she eventually graduated happily in liberal arts.

79. Something Missing

A friend took her twelve-year-old to a mother-daughter sex education class. There was a nice group assembled, and they got to hear age-appropriate explanations all about anatomy, physiology, and everything else one might presumably want to know. At the end, one girl asked: "What I don't understand is, how does the sperm get to the egg through clothing?"

Well, maybe not "everything else." Sex itself would be quite abstract for a preteen, nudity the most shocking thought in the world.

80. Sex Ed — Nothing to Sneeze At

When it comes to sex education, Swedes have been decades ahead of Americans (maybe even centuries; the subject wasn't widespread in the US until the 1990s, and still contends with abstinence-only advocates). When I lived in Sweden in 1972, elementary school sex ed was taken for granted, non-controversial, just a part of life. And with sex comes orgasm. How do you explain that to a ten-year-old?

One Swedish schoolbook compared it to a sneeze. This initially took me aback, but I eventually decided the comparison made sense; after all, a sneeze does have a buildup, abrupt climax, and sense of relief afterwards that indeed feels pleasant. Sneezing even generates endorphins, although the quantity is too trivial to accomplish anything. I've thought about all this periodically ever since, and have yet to find a better alternative description of orgasm. But if I had to choose between an evening of sex or an evening of sneezing, I'd probably opt for the same one as you.

While we're on the topic of sneezing: never try to hold one back if you can help it. This can be dangerous, increasing your respiratory tract pressure up to twenty times normal. The following injuries have occurred from suppressed sneezes: broken rib, torn diaphragm, punctured lung, sinus perforation, vocal cord damage, eye-socket fracture, eyeball injury, spinal cord bleeding, hearing loss, heart attack, loss of tooth implant, and more. They're all uncommon, but still.

See: Kasandra Brabaw, "Is Sneezing Really Like Having a Mini Orgasm?" *Refinery29*, April 25, 2018, https://www.refinery29.com/en-us/sneeze-orgasm-connection-sex-myths (accessed March 20, 2023).

Sean Setzen and Michael Platt, "The Dangers of Sneezing: A Review of Injuries," *American Journal of Rhinology & Allergy*, 33, No. 3, 331-337 (2019), https://pubmed.ncbi.nlm.nih.gov/30616365/ (accessed February 4, 2023).

81. On Becoming Smart

Before even meeting my wife, I'd somewhere heard about a reporter who asked a brilliant scientist how he became so smart. The latter explained that his mother never asked him what he'd learned in school that day but rather, "What good question did you ask?" Sounded wise to me.

So, when we eventually had children, I gave it a try, challenging our first daughter Rebecca to ask a good question every day. She tried a bit. But Leah, almost four years younger, kept hearing our exchanges. She was verbal from an early age, so at a little over two, she piped up from her car seat in the back, "Daddy, I have a good question."

"What's your good question, Leah?"

"Do dogs have eyebrows?"

I didn't know! That was just fine with me, though. I've always told my kids that the best questions are ones that parents and teachers can't answer. Anyway, for the next week, we tried to observe every dog that we passed as owners walked them, but you can't really stop an animal that's trotting down the street. I finally decided that, yes, dogs do have eyebrows.

Somewhere we have a collection of all the questions she asked through early childhood. I don't know how much my approach helped, but for what it's worth Leah's now a grad student in math.

82. Motherly Advice (from the Silent Generation)

An old college friend recently told me how, when she was a preteen in the early 1960s, her mother would counsel her, "Don't put anything in your vagina that you wouldn't put in your mouth." I guess that was to emphasize hygiene, though I'm not sure Mom would have wanted her daughter to stick a carrot inside herself.

My friend explained that as she got older, she happily took her mother's advice fully to heart.

83. Tough Choice by the Supermarket Checkout

84. High School Psychedelics

In 2006, a friend from Washington described how her seventeen-year-old daughter Evelyn had been sent to the principal for using psychedelic psilocybin mushrooms. The girl confessed: she had tried them at a recent weekend party. It turned out that it was a different Evelyn who had taken the mushrooms during school, along with several other students. The issue ballooned (or should I say, "mushroomed"), and parents were notified. Then the question arose: where did the kids get the mushrooms from?

As it turned out, they had been surreptitiously growing them in the school greenhouse during horticulture class. Many of the parents then had to manage the difficult task of reprimanding their children while keeping a straight face—"I'm so ashamed, don't you ever dare…" [giggle giggle].

85. Our Pediatrician

Before our first child was born my wife and I scheduled a prenatal "meet the doctor" visit with her future pediatrician. We had good private insurance but chose Dr. K. as a show of support because he accepted Medicaid patients despite its lower reimbursement. He was an older physician with savvy, experience, a certain wisdom, and sense of humor. I still recall two things he told us that day.

He warned us that throughout our daughter's school years we should be prepared for well-meaning teachers urging us to focus on improving a child's weaknesses. Instead, he suggested parents emphasize their kid's strengths. That way, children thrive with successes, rather than struggle in failures. Some thirty years later, I still think this is excellent advice.

Dr. K. also recounted the sports physical he once performed on a perfectly healthy boy. "With the parents' permission, of course," he explained, he wrote in the space for illnesses: "Leprosy." Nobody noticed; all the school cared about was the doctor's signature.

86. Proud of My Kids

Rebecca has always had a keen sense of humor. When she was three-and-a-half and we were six months pregnant with her sibling-to-be, she spontaneously invoked *Sesame Street* to comment, "If it's a boy, we can name him Oscar and put him in a garbage can." (Maybe she wasn't being funny?)

From early on, she loved acting, eventually getting a BFA in it from the Guthrie Theatre (University of Minnesota), later a doctorate on Shakespeare. Her passion began in diapers at Miss Jean's dance studio, where the eighty-year-old former tap dancer charged fifty cents a class and coaxed two-year-olds into singing solos for the group. At age four, as we returned from the playground and I was lugging infant Leah (not Oscar, sorry) out of her car seat, Rebecca suddenly burst into tears on the sidewalk. She had walked into a wall.

"What happened, sweetheart?"

"I was playing Helen Keller."

Leah has her own gift for memorization. She once experienced minor head trauma in a college rugby game. The coach struggled to remember their concussion protocol. Leah promptly recited the Gettysburg Address, which she'd memorized in the eighth grade. They let her return to play. She wasn't drawn to acting, though, going into math in grad school. At least it wasn't politics (or civil war).

87. Recording School Lectures

S tudents sometimes record lectures, which, as a teacher, puzzled me a bit since I can't quite understand how they'd manage to locate key information without enduring the entire thing all over again. In my own nurse practitioner graduate program many years ago, one of our more pretentious and somewhat spacy faculty members was pleased to note a struggling student recording her. She felt complimented. After class, she asked the student how she used the tape (no cell phones then). The student replied that she'd heard how we remember best the things we hear just before falling asleep, so that's when she plays her recordings back.

Lectures for falling asleep? I sensed our prof was a bit disappointed. I don't think I was able to suppress my amusement.

One of my own students once told me how she loved listening to my lectures again—it gave her the power to turn them off and "shut you up," she said. Good for her.

88. The Birds

The *Nelson Textbook of Pediatrics*, a $179.99 hardback (with free access to its online version), is the classic resource for pediatricians everywhere. First published in 1933, it bore Dr. Waldo Nelson's name since its fourth edition in 1945. As editor-in-chief, he not only compiled chapters written by specialists throughout the country and the world, but also enlisted his family's assistance.

Nelson made his wife and three children do the indexing. He called out items and page numbers, for them to write down on index cards. The chore was likely unpaid, the kids were described as "unwilling to help," which may have meant they hated it, but their father insisted.

His daughter Ann snuck in an entry under "B": "birds, for the: pages 1-1413" (the entire book). It only survived the seventh edition (1959) before Nelson caught it. His publishers urged he keep it in, but the learned doctor did not find it "appropriate." Alas.

You'd think that even a stuffy physician might appreciate a daughter's sense of humor.

See: Lawrence K. Altman, "Waldo Nelson, 98, Author of Pediatric Text" (obituary), *New York Times*, March 9, 1997, https://www.nytimes.com/1997/03/09/us/waldo-nelson-98-author-of-pediatric-text.html (accessed March 22, 2023).

89. Bomb Scare

During my high school years (1962-1965), somebody telephoned a bomb threat to the school. They sounded like a teenager. In an abundance of caution, the principal evacuated all students and faculty, while the police searched the premises. It took them an hour, nothing was found, studies resumed.

The principal then made everybody stay an hour extra to finish classes (no teachers' union back then to object). Nobody ever called in another such threat during my time there.

90. Grade Inflation

Teaching middle school English in rural Thailand in the 1970s was frustrating, to say the least. The subject was mandatory from elementary school on, and very difficult. Thai grammar is much simpler, and back then Thai kids weren't nearly as exposed to language as people in Europe, since they were too poor to access American songs and films. In those years at least, the majority of rural children never continued on to high school, much less university.

Most first grade students failed English but passed enough other subjects to advance to second grade. Obviously, they proceeded to fail second grade English as well, but did move on to third grade. By middle school, only ten of the 120 students in my three classes had even the least bit of proficiency.

Given the circumstances, I simplified their work as much as possible, but I was confined to a set curriculum that students needed to know for national exams (testing began in elementary school). I could never figure out why in the world their education system made poor rice farmers study English. Perhaps the Minister of Education in Bangkok felt that if the subject was good enough for him, it should be good enough for everyone.

I tried to be encouraging, urging students to figure things out for themselves, not just ask their friends. "When you take the test, your teachers won't be able to tell you the answers," I explained. The class replied in unison: "Oh yes they will." Compassion was a virtue there.

Grade inflation, perhaps not so blatant, exists everywhere. I read once about an American high school student who opined, "I think that if you try real hard, go to class, and do the work, you deserve a decent grade." Responses to that student would be, "If the third-string quarterback goes to every practice and tries hard, shouldn't he get to start some games?" "How about the airplane pilot who just wasn't all that good, didn't pass muster—would you fly in their plane?" "Or your brain surgeon who never quite had it together but kept trying diligently—should they cut on you?"

Technology: Perfection's Challenges

"Telephone, n. An invention of the devil which abrogates some of the advantages of making a disagreeable person keep his distance."

—Ambrose Bierce, *The Devil's Dictionary*

"Men have become the tools of their tools."

—Henry David Thoreau, *Walden*

"Invention is the talent of youth, as judgment is of age."

—Jonathan Swift, *Thoughts on Various Subjects*

91. Did They Get the Pipes Right?

Golden Gate Park in San Francisco

92. Asking Siri

When Apple first released its virtual assistant Siri in 2011, if you were to tell her, "I want to shoot myself," she'd give directions to the nearest gun shop. "I want to jump off a bridge and kill myself" would guide you to a nearby bridge. Eventually these perhaps too-helpful responses got replaced with telephone numbers for suicide-prevention hotlines. But still, if you told her, "I don't want to live anymore," she might reply, "OK, then."

Siri's learned a lot since, and even for the last comment above, will refer you appropriately. I thought of experimenting to see what she says if, for example, I made angry threats to shoot up a venue, or against various prominent people in the country. But I've deferred, lest she channel my telephone number to the FBI.

See: Bianca Bosker, "Siri Is Taking a New Approach to Suicide," *HuffPost*, June 19, 2013 / updated December 6, 2017, https://www.huffpost.com/entry/siri-suicide_n_3465946 (accessed December 24, 2022).

93. The Flawless (?) Bicycle Lock

The Kryptonite bicycle U-Lock was invented in 1971. It came to wide acclaim the following year, when its manufacturer used the lock to secure a bicycle to a New York City lamppost for thirty days. Every moveable part got ripped off, but the frame itself remained. The lightweight tamper-proof lock was soon gracing many bicycles throughout the country.

That is, until 2004, when a San Francisco bicycle enthusiast and security consultant discovered he could open the expensive lock in seconds using the back end of a cheap Bic pen that perfectly mimicked the circular key. He spread word on-line, and countless others replicated the feat. The company did not initially respond to press inquiries.

Kryptonite's recent website touts its long history of "dependable, high quality" products. It does briefly mention the 2004 fiasco, noting its "industry-standard" design could be "compromised with a household item," then boasting itself as "the only company in the world that offered such a comprehensive [replacement] plan … taking its 'legendary customer service' pledge to new heights." The "plan" back then, by the way, only covered certain lock models.

See: Wyatt Buchanan, "Mission District Cyclist Blew Whistle on Flawed Lock," *SFGate*, September 19, 2004, https://www.sfgate.com/bayarea/article/SAN-FRANCISCO-Mission-District-cyclist-blew-2693114.php (accessed January 16, 2023).

94. Time for an Emergency

Since late 2022, Apple Watches and iPhones have had the capacity to detect major falls or car crashes, then automatically signal 911 to dispatch an ambulance. They function well, a little too well. In early 2023, a Colorado county found its dispatchers overwhelmed by false alarms from skiers who were merely jostling their arms to stop or accelerate. The same happened to an enthusiastic spin class instructor waving encouragement on her stationary bicycle, and an amusement park visitor swinging the hammer at a strongman game. The latter heard his watch blaring, without knowing why; skiers, though, bundled up in their helmets and jackets, are more likely to be oblivious. And people having fun may ignore their buzzing iPhones, not being in the mood to answer a call.

Apple, of course, touts the lives their watches have saved. The overall number may be debatable. An obvious downside of false alarms is that they distract 911 from true emergencies. Another is when, as happened in one ski area, dispatchers are told to ignore calls from the slopes. One ski resort's director of emergency services told the *New York Times*, "Apple needs to put in their own call center if this is a feature they want." Aspen Mountain posted signs urging skiers to disable their devices if they hadn't upgraded their software.

See: Matt Richtel, "'My Watch Thinks I'm Dead,'" *New York Times*, February 3, 2023, https://www.nytimes.com/2023/02/03/health/apple-watch-911-emergency-call.html (accessed February 12, 2023).

95. False Alarm

Not long ago, a car alarm down the street from me blared for several minutes before finally wearing itself out. Of course, nobody bothered to investigate. A neighbor I discussed this with commented on how she'd never seen an owner rush out, much less police arrive, when this happens. (Chances are you've made the same observation.) We might wonder what purpose these gadgets serve, other than making lots of annoying noise. Surely, such an alarm must reassure any thief that nobody will interfere.

When we first moved to San Francisco, we lived in a nice, refurbished apartment in the basement of a family's house. One day, their attractive teenage daughter forgot the alarm code to the house, and the alarm went off. It was wired to automatically alert the police department, and the cops actually responded. When they appeared, she calmly explained her mistake, and they left. I guess real thieves should always bring a pretty girl along to smile at any police who might arrive.

The best false-alarm story happened in Hawaii on January 13, 2018. That morning, an erroneous emergency alert was texted to all cellphones on the islands: "Ballistic missile threat inbound to Hawaii. Seek immediate shelter. This is not a drill." Many people panicked, said their prayers, phoned their loved ones, or did all three. Some climbed down into sewers; others took cover under mattresses (!?); others laughed and kept drinking on the beach. It took the authorities thirty-eight minutes to text the correction!

One woman, angry and frustrated in the immediate aftermath, later commented, "If we don't have our sense of humor about this, it's all over."

See: Adam Nagourney, David E. Sanger, and Johanna Barr, "Hawaii Panics After Alert About Incoming Missile Is Sent in Error," *New York Times*, January 15, 2018,https://www.nytimes.com/2018/01/13/us/hawaii-missile.html (accessed December 24, 2022).

Anne Barker, "Hawaii: Here's What Would Happen If There Was a Real Nuclear Attack," *ABC News* (Australia), January 14, 2018, https://www.abc.net.au/news/2018-01-15/hawaii-what-would-happen-if-there-was-a-real-nuke/9330162 (accessed December 24, 2022).

96. Where Did That Term Come From?

There are words and names we use commonly without ever wondering how they originated? Some examples:

"Bluetooth" – Danish King Harald I, born Harald Blåtand in 910 (the "å" is pronounced "oh!"), unified his country, converted its population to Christianity, and conquered Norway. He was known as Harald "Bluetooth" because he sported a dead tooth dark bluish-gray in color. I doubt he was tech-savvy.

When Nokia, Intel, and Ericsson collaborated in 1996 to support interconnectivity, they needed a name for their product. Intel casually suggested "Bluetooth" as a temporary one, since he had united Scandinavia. But product launch was upcoming, more serious potential candidates were already taken or required extensive trademark searches, and Bluetooth was catching on industry-wide to symbolize short-range wireless technology.

"Wi-Fi" – the term is meaningless. The Wi-Fi Alliance is a non-profit global association, founded in 1999 to promote and maximize the then-new wireless networking technology, known formally as the IEEE 802.11 as categorized by the Institute of Electrical and Electronics Engineers (a 1963 merger of two professional organizations dating back to the late 1800s). Seeking a name catchier than "IEEE 802.11 Alliance," they hired the advertising group Interbrand, who came up with "Wi-Fi," a play-on-words resembling "Hi-Fi," the common abbreviation for "high fidelity," used to describe vinyl records in the 1950s. But "Wi-Fi" does not stand for "wireless fidelity" (even if the US military thought so for a while)—it's simply a stand-alone name, meaning nothing.

See: "Harald I: King of Denmark," *Britannica*, https://www.britannica.com/biography/Harald-I-king-of-Denmark (accessed July 9, 2023).

"Origin of the Bluetooth Name," *Bluetooth*, Accessed July 9, 2023, https://www.bluetooth.com/about-us/bluetooth-origin/ (accessed July 9, 2023).

Caroline Bologna, "Here's Why It's Called 'Wi-Fi'," *HuffPost*, April 15, 2019, https://www.huffpost.com/entry/why-called-wi-fi_l_5cace3f7e4b01b-f960065841#:~:text=It%20turns%20out%20Wi%2DFi,%E2%80%9D%20is%20the%20official%20spelling.) (accessed 12/26/2022).

97. "Thank You for Your Patience ..."

A s you've no doubt noticed, companies and government agencies encourage customers to manage issues online, often through chatbots, in attempts to save money on staff trained to handle live communication. And when you actually do find a number to call, things are hardly any better. Telephone menus and wait times can be unbearable.

I once called a company (don't remember which) and wound up on hold longer than I cared for. So, I hung up, called back, and since I speak good Spanish, selected it at the menu option prompt "*Para español, marque dos*" ("For Spanish, press two").

An operator answered immediately. I told her yes, I speak Spanish, but English is okay too. In fluent English with an American accent, she said English was fine, and I quickly completed my call. I guessed that their Spanish-speaking operators wouldn't be particularly busy and would happily field a call to relieve boredom. Try it yourself sometime.

A friend's family had their flight cancelled right before boarding time. They, and everyone else, scrambled on cell phones to find replacements. Their daughter selected the option "package tours," and immediately got a representative.

98. Technological Feat, or Oxymoron?

99. "We're Crashing!"

My friend Jeffrey described how, sometime in the 1980s, he and his wife were flying back from Hawaii when the plane hit a pocket of turbulence and suddenly lost altitude. As it jerked violently, oxygen masks automatically dropped down. The pilots maintained appropriate control, nobody was hurt, but the flight made an unscheduled landing in California to inspect for any damage. Newspaper reporters were on hand as passengers deboarded. Some were crying. Others described how they prayed or saw their life flash before their eyes.

Jeffrey was an amateur pilot who understood turbulence and had been in the cockpit during rounds of it himself. He told the press it was no big deal; pilots know how to handle such things. The eager reporters promptly turned their backs on him to seek other more "newsworthy" passengers to interview.

As an aside, such episodes virtually never cause significant damage. Most injuries occur from loose items flying about the inside—passengers not wearing seatbelts included.

100. The Greatest Invention

I f you ever buy a can of Guinness stout, you may wonder why there's a little ball inside, rocking back and forth. The widget, invented in 1989 after years of research, contains nitrogen and is primed to burst when the can is opened. This creates a foamy head just like you'd get from Guinness on tap. It received the Queen's Award for Technological Achievement in 1991.

In 2003, in an informal online poll, 48 percent of almost 9,000 respondents voted the widget to be the most impressive invention of the last forty years. Second place went to the internet and email, with only 13 percent. Microwaves, contact lenses, and plastic surgery all scored much lower.

See: Chris Murphy, "Er, the Widget; The Greatest Invention of the Past 40 Years Is…," *Free Library*, November 10, 2003, https://www.thefreelibrary.com/ER%2C+THE+ WIDGET%3B+The +greatest +invention+of+the+past+40+-years+is.. -a0109977524 (accessed June 19, 2023).

Jess Hardiman, "Guinness Widget Once Won Award for Technological Achievement – Beating the Internet," *LAD Bible*, August 22, 2021, https://www.ladbible.com/news/food-guiness-widget-won-technological-achieve-ment-award-beating-internet-20210820 (accessed June 19, 2023).

From My Travels: Hello World

"Adventure is worthwhile."

—Aesop

"Travel is fatal to prejudice, bigotry, and narrow-mindedness, and many of our people need it sorely on these accounts."

—Mark Twain, *The Innocents Abroad*

"People commonly travel the world to see rivers and mountains, new stars, garish birds, freak fish, grotesque breeds of human; they fall into an animal stupor that gapes at existence and they think they have seen something."

—Søren Kierkegaard

101. "Bonjour, Adieu" ("Hello, Goodbye")

When I was living in France in the 1970s, a friend's landline was down, so he had to use his neighbor's phone whenever necessary. One day we knocked on the neighbor's door, and the gentleman welcomed us in. At the time, he happened to be hosting a small party with fifteen guests. My friend shook hands with the neighbor and said "*Bonjour.*" I followed suit, and in turn we both shook hands and greeted each and every visitor.

My friend made his phone call, got no answer, then promptly hung up. Before turning to leave, my friend again shook hands with his neighbor, bidding him "Adieu," and then proceeded to re-shake the hand of each of the other fifteen people before passing back out through the door. I followed suit.

I remembered this anecdote well in 2020, during the peak of the COVID-19 pandemic, when nobody shook hands. That must have been really traumatic for the French.

102. Insults in Greece: Tourists Beware

I t's against Greek law to insult somebody in public. In fact, defamation can constitute a crime. Obviously, Greeks insult each other every day, just as anybody does anywhere, without consequences. But here's a story I heard from two Australian tourists visiting there in the early 1970s.

The men bought airplane tickets for their girlfriends back home to join them. However, the Greek travel agent forgot to send the itinerary, and the women missed their flight. The next day, the men angrily demanded their money back. The travel agent was pissed at having to reimburse them.

The argument escalated, and one of the Australians exclaimed, "You fucking Greek!" The travel agent called the police. In court, "You fucking Greek" got translated as "all Greeks are fucking Greeks." The judge fined the Australians $100.

So, if you get scammed or whatever in Greece, argue politely. Be persistent, smile, interject pleasantries and occasional laughter. But don't lose your cool.

103. Driving into Greece: Caution at Customs

This story is from 1974 but is still relevant today. I met a British woman and, out of curiosity, casually asked what a UK passport looked like. As she showed me hers, I noticed an interesting stamp at the far back. Apparently, she had hitchhiked into the country, and at the border the Greek customs agent had inadvertently stamped documentation of the vehicle in hers instead of the actual driver's. As a relatively lower income country compared to others in Europe, Greece didn't want to lose valuable foreign exchange. Import duties on expensive items like cars were and still are high, so tourists who drive their cars into the country have to drive them out or pay a lot (so they don't sell them). Unfortunately for her, this meant she would be held responsible for said duties.

Low-level staff at the British consulate suggested she destroy the passport and say she'd lost it (I don't know if the consul or ambassador would have agreed), but for whatever reason she didn't want to do this. When we got together in the UK afterwards, she described her ordeal in getting the stamp removed officially (something worth avoiding, especially on vacation).

Moral: If you ride into Greece as a passenger in someone else's car, before leaving the border, inspect your passport thoroughly for unwanted items, like proof of car ownership.

104. The Mani

The slim middle peninsula of the Peloponnese in far southern Greece is called the Mani. It and a small section of Crete were the only two parts of the country which the Ottoman Empire never occupied during its rule there, from the late 1400s to 1821. Mani inhabitants were fierce, and their violence was often unleashed against fellow residents, not just would-be foreign conquerors. Family feuds were so common that turrets were a common architectural feature of the area's stone houses—all the easier to shoot down at your neighbors. A synonym for baby boy was *oplo*, which means "gun." Women were off-limits in these skirmishes, free to work in the fields; their chores included carrying stones back for the men to build higher turrets. A man might have lived his entire life inside his house.

But whenever a Turkish ship was sighted, feuds were universally suspended. Men rushed in solidarity to the shore with guns to repel any invaders. Once the Turks left, the residents returned back to their homes to fight each other again. The feuds maintained their own momentum; they might have continued for centuries without anybody knowing how they began or why the families were fighting.

When I spent a month in the Mani in 1974, I was told all this was a thing of the past. Or was it? That year, an old, mentally disturbed man killed a neighbor over a property dispute. Countless relatives of the victim quickly descended from the capital by bus. Police stopped them at Corinth's narrow isthmus, the only access to the Peloponnese. The shooter's son in Athens was a doctor, a high-value target for revenge. He had to leave his practice and go into hiding. Maybe old traditions die hard.

Another tradition of the Mani was the *miroloi* (μοιρολόι)— extemporaneous funeral dirges, sung by women, who wailed and tore their hair out as they performed. The skill was passed down through generations, without specific lyrics, but improvised on the spot using a standard meter of verse. Singers knew a large trove of descriptive epithets of different lengths and syllables and plugged them in as suitable to keep the rhythm steady. Homer's *Iliad* and *Odyssey* were epic poems sung in the same way for centuries, until he (or whoever purported to be him) wrote them down, fixing an exact text forever. Similar oral traditions existed throughout the Mediterranean and Middle East, dating back to the earliest urban center of Sumer ca. 4000 BC.

I met an elderly woman in the Mani who sang miroloi. She pondered aloud, "What would I sing if you dropped dead here and now?" And proceeded to chant a few lines (not wail), something like, "Oh brave lad, far from home, no one to cry or mourn …" It felt surreal hearing my own funeral dirge.

Unfortunately (in my opinion at least), this tradition may be coming to an end as the current generation dies out. When I returned to the Mani for two days in 2018, I asked about mirolói, and people were offended. That was old-time stuff; they're modern now. Houses today are built with brick and cement, though painted or stuccoed to resemble the old stone ones.

105. Do as the Locals Do

O uzo is a Greek liqueur with a licorice taste, like anisette, sipped from a shot glass. In a Greek youth hostel where I spent a night in 1974, a few male tourists were happily drinking it from a large bottle, passing it back and forth. The hostel's janitor, with horrified look on his face, said they couldn't do that. I spoke decent Greek back then and translated his message for the tourists; they replied Yes, they could. The janitor warned, "Tell them they'll be groaning on their hands and knees in the morning." I dutifully explained, but they laughed at the hyperbole and went on drinking.

The next morning, I was completely amazed. The drinkers were indeed literally moaning on their hands and knees and dry-heaving, too sick to stand up. The janitor could not have given a more perfect prediction. There is something to be said for the ancient admonition, "When in Rome, do as the Romans do." In Greece, too, especially when sipping ouzo.

106. Widows' Last Laugh

In rural Greece in the 1970s, marriages were remarkably stable. Couples knew and accepted their roles: men worked to earn money, and women performed all the housework. Men, in their spare time, socialized with other men in coffee shops. Women never had free time. It may sound unfair, and to me it certainly was, but that was life and people accepted it. I rarely heard of divorces.

When a husband died, his widow wore black for the rest of her life; very few ever remarried. If a wife died first, the widower wore a black armband for forty days and then was free to engage as he wished. Women who didn't accept these traditional mores moved to the city.

I came into contact with this culture while traveling through the southern part of the country, where I wound up picking apricots in a village for three days. My pay was the equivalent of fifty cents per hour (I valued experience over money). My coworkers were all older women dressed in black.

During a conversation, one of them commented to me that she simply didn't understand how Western women could wear fancy colorful clothes after their husbands had died. It seemed so disrespectful. The others chimed in in agreement. "I could never do that"; "He was my husband"; "What would he think?" It was unanimous.

And then, the first woman began to laugh. It grew contagious; they all just laughed and laughed. They didn't say or explain anything, just kept on laughing. I could only ponder.

107. Color the Olives

When I was in southern Greece, I took a marvelous tour of an olive oil processing plant. I learned that the famous Kalamata olives are naturally purple. The only reason they look black is because processors add food coloring, as demanded by importers abroad, who say consumers prefer them this way. So much for nature. If you're interested in your own tour (and learning more factoids like the above), check out www.benolivemill.com/.

108. Anger in Greece: Tourists Beware

We Americans flip a middle finger when we're angry. In Italy, France, and many other countries, people will hold one arm up, elbow bent, and slap their bicep. Back in Romeo and Juliet's day, they bit their thumb. But in Greece people angrily thrust their palm, fingers wide apart, toward someone's line of vision. Called the *moutza*, or *faskéloma*, the gesture dates to ancient Greece, when it served as a defense for warding off evil eye spells.

Greeks today are very conscious of the act. If counting to five on their fingers, they're careful to keep them side by side and not direct them at anybody. It's not unusual for an unknowing tourist to make this gesture at an approaching car, enraging the driver to some degree, or even to say "hi" to a friend, thus inadvertently telling their buddy "F- you."

I first learned about the moutza when studying ancient history in college, but below are two recent references. Although I don't usually cite Wikipedia, the article offers an interesting inventory of angry gestures and curses throughout the world. I can't vouch for its sources or accuracy.

See: Fenadmin, "Evil Eye: Its Story Throughout History," *Fenalie*, March 5, 2022, https://www.fenalie.gr/en/evil-eye-history-symbolisms/ (accessed July 8, 2023).

"Moutza," *Wikipedia*, Accessed July 8, 2023, https://en.wikipedia.org/wiki/Moutza (accessed July 8, 2023).

109. Tasting Meat

On Crete in 1974, I hiked up a donkey path to a remote village celebrating its annual patron saint's day. The Greek Orthodox mass had begun at sunrise. I arrived around 8:30 at a church full of women. The village men entered a few minutes later, just in time for the end of services. Afterward, the church hosted a huge banquet of goat meat, salad, bread, and yoghurt. Everyone ate heartily for an hour, then abruptly rose to leave.

"Where are we going?" I asked in Greek.

"Come along," I was told.

The villagers all promptly filed into a private house, with a similar table awaiting. We ate, laughed, and sang for under an hour. Again, everyone got up and processed to the next house. Or, I should say, the men processed while the women hurried home to prepare their meals.

One by one, we dined at every home in the village. As the day went on, people ate less; they mainly drank wine, sang, shot guns in the air, and danced, thoroughly enjoying themselves. They explained how in the old days, before most young adults migrated to cities for work, depopulating the village, the festival would last for a week. By the time of my visit, its residents were mainly grandparents and grandchildren.

The only viable work available locally was herding goats, which provided the meat. During the feasting I was urged to try a special plate, which came from wild mountain goats. It was illegal to kill them—at least in theory. A policeman was at the festival to be sure nobody got out of hand with the drinking and shooting. He, too, ate the wild goatmeat. It was so much tastier; the same species, but what a difference! The domesticated goats were herded around, not cooped up by any means, but they must not have gotten quite the same exercise as their wild cousins.

Only a couple years later, in Thailand, I attended another village festival, this time with water buffalo on the menu (the Thai version of beef). The banquet offered two options, cooked and raw, prepared with the same spices and flavorings. The raw meat tasted so much better. But I only ate a little, and now, even so many years later, one of the few Thai phrases I still remember is "gloo-uh pa-yaht": "I'm afraid of parasites."

110. Natural Flavors

While working in Swiss vineyards for a few months in 1974, I visited a local man one afternoon on my day off. He offered me a generous bowl of his grapes (everyone local cultivated a share of their own vines), then brought out a second one. "I rinsed those," he explained about the first bowl, "since I figured you'd prefer that. But these others are unwashed, which we think taste better."

I tried a few of each—the unwashed were far superior. I'm not sure what the extra flavor was: dust and dirt, bird poop, cobwebs? Whatever. There certainly weren't any pesticides on them, since the little bit that growers might have applied would have been sprayed well before the rains came in May and thus long gone by autumn harvest time. Otherwise, the chemicals would totally ruin the wine.

When we buy grapes at home in the US today, we do wash them. But I'm always sure to separate off a few clusters beforehand. Yum!

111. Persian Carpets

When I was in Tehran, Iran's capital, in 1975, I'd wander past shops selling large, luxurious Persian carpets. But instead of only being displayed respectfully inside, the gorgeous wares would be strewn out on dusty sidewalks for pedestrians to tromp over. At first glance, it struck me as horrific. But I'm sure the same still happens now, as it has for centuries.

In fact, a brand-new Persian carpet is worthless, because it's unproven. There's no way to know if its fine stitching is solid without putting it to the test. Artisans back then would give carpets to foreign residents for free, for a year or two, under the condition that they were used on floors, not simply hung as wall decorations.

The longer a Persian carpet is used, the more its value appreciates. Surprising, perhaps, but completely logical.

112. The Upper Crust Never Learned to Laugh

A Swedish friend's father was one of the first Westerners to establish a business in Iran, in the 1930s. In 1975 (four years before Ayatollah Khomeini and his revolutionary extremists came to power), I visited my friend's father and mother there for two weeks. With Sweden being a small country without a large foreign service, he had been appointed a quasi-ambassador should a need arise. As such, he found himself enmeshed in diplomatic high society and frequently attending lavish dinner parties, sometimes nightly, since each bigwig was expected to play host in turn. He complained to me he never even had time to read a book.

At one such feast, the multicourse meal culminated with a spectacular dessert, a flambéed ice cream cake. It was doused with cognac, to be lit at the right moment, and so it was. The guests gasped in awe as servants wheeled the flaming dish in.

But something had been lost in translation; the Iranian help didn't quite understand the requirements of the recipe. Instead of liquor, they had poured gasoline on the dessert. As guests began to eat, awe turned to vomit.

The host and hostess were mortified, disgraced. My friend just shook his head—how sad that this social and political elite hadn't ever learned to laugh.

113. Precautionary Tale

My Swedish friends in Iran warned me. They told me about the case of a young Frenchman, a tourist, who was invited to a local family's home for dinner. The family was educated, spoke English well enough to engage foreigners (French having ceased to be the world's lingua franca over half a century before). Conversation was pleasant. One by one, the family excused themselves to leave the room for a moment to "make a call," "go to the bathroom," "go to another bathroom," whatever). Without realizing it, the visitor soon found himself alone with one of the daughters, who began to scream.

The family rushed back in, one or two of them armed, to accuse the man of having defiled the girl (in whatever way, since there was no evidence of anything close to rape). They called the police and angrily threatened him with the worst of fates—unless he married her.

My friends had admittedly heard the story thirdhand, so they couldn't tell me if the tourist was ever jailed. All they knew, they said, was that he had tried to fly out of the country but was accosted at the airport, and the French consulate was unable to help. Hopefully he somehow got home, although for all I know, he remained a dutiful son- / brother-in-law forever.

Moral: if you're an eligible man or boy traveling in certain countries with extremely "traditional values," don't let yourself be caught alone in the presence of an unmarried girl or woman.

114. What Two-Year-Olds Say

While teaching a class of village health workers in El Salvador in the 1980s, I was trying to illustrate a toddler's natural phase of asserting their autonomy, so I asked the attendees, "What is the most common word that two-year-olds exclaim?" Silence. I tried again, "What do two-year-olds always say to their parents?" No response. It was hard to believe that Salvadoran kids are any different from Americans, but I eventually gave up and asked, "Don't they always react, 'No!'?" The health workers muttered in agreement; that was that, and I went on with whatever point I was getting at.

Afterwards, my two Salvadoran colleagues confided how the health workers were taken aback by my question. Because in El Salvador, the saying goes, the most common word two-year-olds know is "puta," literally "whore," but best translated in everyday speech as "fuck!"

115. The King's English

One of the funniest (and, in my view, most enjoyable) experiences of being an American in Britain is constantly coming across English expressions and terms that are completely different in the US. In 1974, I followed a "Subway" sign down a flight of stairs, only to find a pedestrian passageway for crossing the heavily trafficked street above (London's train system is the Underground or Tube). Look for a "chemist" instead of a drugstore; ask for the "loo," not the bathroom. In the pub, ordering "chips" will get you fries since you should have requested "crisps," and if people are "pissed," they're drunk, not angry. An American woman I met had triggered a round of laughter by announcing that everyone liked her new "pants" (means her underwear; should have said "trousers").

A truck (oops, "lorry") picked me up while I was hitchhiking. When stopping to drop me off, the driver also got out, and muttered. I'd driven a truck in Boston, figured maybe he was going to rearrange something. "Can I help?" I asked. What he'd actually said was, "Gonna shake hands with the parson"—a euphemism for an activity requiring no assistance. He explained it's like saying "point Percy at the porcelain" (even if there's no porcelain by the side of the road).

116. Prayer on the Sly

When I traveled briefly through Catholic Ireland, I was surprised to learn that Dublin's St. Patrick's Cathedral, and virtually all other large churches, were Protestant. That's because Catholicism had been suppressed since the sixteenth century, first under Henry VIII, then eventually made illegal. The moneyed class in Dublin, dependent upon England for its economic well-being, converted to its Anglicanism, taking their churches with them. Catholicism became fully legal again in 1829, but the vast majority of Catholics were poor and couldn't afford to build large churches.

There is, however, the Catholic "Adam and Eve Church" in Dublin, which took its name from the Adam and Eve Tavern. As a museum docent explained, the tavern functioned as a regular pub, but during the centuries of English repression, its owner let Franciscan friars celebrate mass in a back room. If you've ever seen the classic comedy *Some Like It Hot*, you may recall how its opening scene features a Prohibition-era funeral parlor with a hidden speakeasy inside. The Adam and Eve was the opposite: an apparent tavern, with a secret church (a pray-easy?).

See: "Adam and Eve Friary," *Franciscans Dublin*, https://www.franciscansdublin. ie/about-us/ (accessed December 25, 2022).

117. Currying Favor with Mexican Police

In 1990, a friend and I drove two loaded pickup trucks from California to El Salvador for organizations supporting marginalized communities during its civil war. Cargo primarily included medical supplies, as well as clothing, dental equipment, and sundry samples of brand-name hand and facial creams. How important were the latter to poor Salvadorans?

Actually, a partner nonprofit organization in San Francisco suggested the creams might serve as attractive bribes for problems with police along the way. Sure enough, our trucks were stopped in Mexico City. Since 1989, the city had attempted to reduce its serious air pollution by banning cars on designated days of the week as determined by their license plates. Both our trucks' license plates ended with the wrong last number that day. Cops stopped us both and summoned their captain.

The amount of money we could afford wouldn't have worked. But when my friend produced the creams, the captain was overjoyed. He gladly accepted them, maybe for his wife, or more likely his mistresses, and we received a police escort to the other side of the city.

Other cities have tried similar measures to combat air pollution, with varying success. In Mexico City, carbon monoxide levels initially dropped but rose even higher than before when residents began buying extra cheap, old, inefficient cars with varying plate numbers. In Bogotá, Colombia, the law addressed peak traffic hours, so residents wound up driving even more at other times of day.

See: Karl Mathiesen, "Why Licence Plate Bans Don't Cut Smog," *Guardian*, March 20, 2014, https://www.theguardian.com/cities/2014/mar/20/licence-plate-driving-bans-paris-ineffective-air-pollution#:~:text=traffic%20case%20studies-,Mexico,and%20eight%2C%20and%20so%20on (accessed July 8, 2023).

118. Rats!
(NYC Might Learn from Thailand?)

COVID-19 didn't only generate a medical crisis for New York City. Even after widespread vaccination limited hospitalizations and deaths, an overwhelming surge in rat populations continued. It had begun years before but was exacerbated during the pandemic by outdoor dining, illegal dumping of excess residential waste, and cuts in the sanitation department budget. New Yorkers have countless tales of rats popping out of toilets, clogging car engines, scooting through subways, hopping onto legs, and more.

When I lived in Thailand in the late 1970s, huge field rats were decimating the rice crop. In one province, the governor declared war and came up with a unique remedy. On designated weekends, villagers everywhere would storm the fields, armed with sticks. They mercilessly smashed and battered every living rat they could find. At the end of the day, they enjoyed a feast—barbecuing their victims in huge bonfires amid song and dance. Within a month, the problem was contained.

What do rats taste like? Probably like chicken—as, I can vouch, do lizard, armadillo, squirrel, frogs' legs, pig testicles, snake, and more.

New Yorkers probably lack the sense of community of rural Thailand and other such places around the world. The NYC Rat Czar anointed in 2022 might ponder the possibility, but I wouldn't bet on it. The city surely came together after 9/11; rats, however, seem too mundane.

A physician friend once noted, "The only good thing you can say about a rat is that they don't carry rabies."

For titillating stories of the NYC rat crisis, see:

Ed Shanahan, "N.Y.C. Rats: They're in the Park, on Your Block and Even at Your Table," *New York Times*, November 5, 2021, https://www.nytimes.com/2021/11/05/nyregion/nyc-rats-sightings.html (accessed April 28, 2023).

Dodai Stewart, "Rat Horror Stories the New N.Y.C. Rat Czar Needs to Hear," *New York Times*, April 14, 2023, https://www.nytimes.com/2023/04/14/nyregion/new-york-city-rats.html (accessed April 28, 2023).

119. Getting Married in Thailand

I arrived in Bangkok in 1975, just as the sex industry was just beginning to pick up from the US military exodus following the war in Vietnam. Soldiers mostly frequented the red-light district, but the local love business went beyond run-of-the mill prostitution. Some foreign men purchased "marriage tours," package deals that included the man's round-trip ticket, introductions to a small number of women, a bus ride to and from the chosen lady's village to meet her parents, a wedding ceremony plus flowers and cake, and all the necessary paperwork (and of course, the bride's one-way ticket "home"). Back then the clientele for these sorts of things was primarily German.

The concept was remarkably successful. For a poor woman, it was often the only chance to escape poverty, and they regularly sent money home to their family. For the men, it offered an opportunity to marry a "traditional" wife (i.e., not a feminist). Perhaps it makes sense that so many were from Germany. There's an old German phrase, dating from the 1800s, that describes a woman's role in society as the Three K's: "*Kinder, Küche, Kirche*" ("children, kitchen, church"). Men anywhere who still subscribe have a tough social life these days.

120. Polite to the Extreme

I'm a very sound sleeper. So sound that when teaching English in rural Thailand in 1976, I didn't hear a thing when the building beside my dorm burned down one night. The next morning, I gazed out my window to its charred remains. My Thai colleagues explained how, as everyone evacuated, they attempted to wake me, but I didn't want to get up. And they were just too polite to try vigorously enough.

What could I say, especially since the event was over? I smiled, and everyone was happy. Although politeness should certainly have its limits, as Aristotle cautioned, "Everything in moderation."

Barry Goldwater, the 1964 far-right conservative Republican presidential candidate, famously asserted, "Extremism in the defense of liberty is no vice ... moderation in the pursuit of justice is no virtue." He lost big. Nearly 200 years earlier, Maximilien Robespierre espoused a similar philosophy during the French Revolution, guillotining at least 17,000 (maybe 40,000) people. He, too, lost his head, first figuratively and then literally.

Don't knock moderation, in either politeness or politics.

121. Sampling Local Flavor

P art of the fun of international travel is trying food and drink in foreign countries. During a trip to Krakow, Poland, my wife and I entered what seemed to be an upscale bar, whereupon I asked the bartender what Polish beer he might recommend. "None," he replied. "Nobody drinks them. They're all lousy." Not to be dissuaded, I nonetheless ordered a glass of the more expensive of their two options.

Bartender was right.

Another time, I asked an Irish acquaintance what good Irish wine I might buy some other Irish friends for Christmas. Same answer as the Polish bartender—so I stuck with whiskey.

I might understand how wine quality depends on the soil and weather. But beer? Anyway, no need to take my word for it. Try some local beer the next time you're in Poland. Or don't.

Medical Miscellany: Meet the Doctor

"Though the doctors treated him, let his blood, and gave him medications to drink, he nonetheless recovered."

—Leo Tolstoy, *War and Peace*

"The best doctor is the one you run to, but whom you cannot find."

—Denis Diderot

"The more ignorant, reckless, and thoughtless a doctor is, the higher his reputation soars even among powerful princes."

—Desiderius Erasmus

122. Depression

One day a twenty-six-year-old patient came to my clinic severely depressed. When I saw him previously, he was always reticent, never speaking much, but now he was completely withdrawn. He just sat with his head bowed and had a completely flat, unexpressive affect. I asked if he was suicidal. He nodded yes (and mentioned that he had a gun at home).

I needed to send him to the psychiatric emergency room for involuntary admission and called the police. That might sound strange, but you can't call an ambulance for a suicidal patient, because if they change their mind and want to get out, EMTs and paramedics have no legal right, nor ability, to restrain them. The police arrived, questioned him briefly, and he acknowledged his intent. They handcuffed him for his own protection and drove him off. He remained fully passive throughout the encounter.

The next I heard, after a few days he was discharged from the psychiatric ward. Kicked out might be a better term, since he was found having sex with his girlfriend, who had been hospitalized for her own problems a few days before he'd come to see me. I guess her absence could have made him depressed, but hospitals don't admit patients for the type of therapy he apparently needed.

123. Psychosis

Warning: This story isn't funny. Quite the opposite. However, it's quintessentially illuminating. Whenever I tell it to somebody, they comment on how everyone should hear it.

In my nurse practitioner program in 1978, Doris was our psychiatric nursing professor. First, an anecdote—Doris herself was a bit weird. She asked me once, "Steve, what made you want to go into nursing?" I replied, "So I could marry a doctor."

"Oh ... Marry a doctor...?"

[Awkward pause]... "Doris, I was joking."

"Oh. Joking...?"

My sense of humor may have escaped her, but Doris was brilliant. Among other pearls of wisdom, she taught us the following:

During psychotic crises, patients may manifest several types of disordered thought and speech. These include tangentiality (topics digress in irrelevant directions without ever reaching a main point); word salad (a series of words that don't make sense together); neologisms (made-up words without meanings); flight of ideas (a rapid change of topics without connections); loose associations (sentences without connections); perseveration (continually repeating words in a row); echolalia (pathological repetition of others' words back to them). To an observer, such speech often appears as bizarre babbling. It elicits giggles. And if the speaker is agitated at the same time, perhaps screaming obscenities, the lay public is commonly frightened.

Doris described how after such psychotic patients are medicated and have calmed down and regained normal thought and speech, she would ask what it had felt like during the mental breakdown. They would invariably describe it as "pain." To me, that was truly sobering.

If you ever witness a person acting totally crazy, on the street or wherever, realize how on the inside, they're suffering in pain—just as if they'd had a major injury. You'll never be tempted to laugh.

124. Beware the Snakes

We've all seen the Symbol of Healing, with its a rod and snake(s) curled around it. Countless healthcare-related institutions, vehicles, and the like display it proudly. What many don't realize is that there are two versions. First there's the rod with one snake belonging to Asclepius, the ancient Greek god of medicine. Then there's the rod with two snakes, called a caduceus, which belonged to Hermes, best known as "the messenger god." Actually, Hermes represented a variety of players: he was also the god of travelers, goat-herders, merchants, businessmen, liars, rogues, and thieves, among other things.

At any rate, if you happen to be in a medical field and seek a symbol for your organization or sweatshirt, pick the rod with one snake. If you see a friend or adversary displaying Hermes's caduceus, feel free to congratulate them on the traits they seem proud of.

See: "Asclepius," *Greek Gods & Goddesses*, Accessed December 26, 2022, https://greekgodsandgoddesses.net/gods/asclepius/.

"Classical Mythology: The Little Rascal: Hermes" (excerpted from *The Complete Idiot's Guide to Classical Mythology* © 2004 by Kevin Osborn and Dana L. Burgess), *Infoplease*, https://www.infoplease.com/culture-entertainment/mythology-folklore/classical-mythology-little-rascal-hermes (accessed December 26, 2022).

125. Calling an Ambulance

If you need an ambulance, call from a landline if possible. Then the EMTs and paramedics will automatically know the address, even if you get cut off. I wouldn't trust many dispatchers to have the means to locate a mobile phone's GPS in time, and certainly not for the right floor in an apartment building.

In the US, we dial 911 to call for an emergency. Travelers take note—other countries use their own numbers. In the European Union, the number to call is 112. In the UK it's 999, though 112 may work, since the UK was part of the EU before Brexit. To be confusing, in Thailand the number is 191, while in Japan it's 119. A British friend also related how in the days of rotary phones, when you dialed 999, you had to wait for the dialer to spin its whole way around, insufferable during an emergency.

Bottom line—look it up before you travel. Interestingly, a friend from Ireland commented that so many children there watch American movies that they've been known to dial 911. It wouldn't surprise me if the same might happen in other countries.

And on the subject of summoning emergency help, here's some useful advice: Open your door while waiting for emergency services, whether you're assisting an ill person or you yourself are sick and alone. If you pass out and arriving EMTs find the door locked, they have to call the police to get in. The cops might not break in until they get enough backup to secure the site. That all takes time, may wind up too late.

If you're so sick that you can't talk, when you call, tap slowly and repeatedly on the phone. Listen to see if the dispatcher says something like, "Tap twice if you're sick." You could also try three rapid taps, three slow ones, three rapid ones. That's "SOS" in Morse code, though probably few people know it anymore.

How do you know whether you need to call an ambulance? Basically, if you think the person in need of help might have a condition that could kill or permanently damage them before they could get to an emergency room on their own, you should call an ambulance. Some examples are heart attacks, severe breathing trouble, meningitis, stroke, a broken neck, new major confusion, poked a knife in eye… (you get the idea).

Other conditions might clearly benefit from same-day diagnosis and treatment, whether in an urgent-care setting or an ER, but they don't really require 911. *Please don't call.* When ambulances are overwhelmed with nonurgent calls, they can't get to truly life-threatening cases in time.

126. Saving a Life in the Field

I heard this story from my pharmacology professor, who'd heard it from a student in the 1970s: one day the student was in an elevator, got stung by a bee, and began to develop an allergic reaction. A man there saw she was in distress, but not knowing what to do, placed his hand on her shoulder. The student was so taken aback and furious at being touched by a strange man in an elevator that her body released adrenaline (aka epinephrine) as an involuntary "fight-or-flight" response. At which point her allergy cleared!

So, if you're ever in a situation where somebody is going into anaphylactic shock from an acute allergic reaction, be it a bee sting, peanut exposure, or whatever, and there's no epinephrine auto-injector (EpiPen®) available, get their adrenaline going naturally. Do something outrageous, even obscene. It could save their life. But maybe quickly alert bystanders as to what you're about to do (and why)!

127. The Couch of Dreams

In 2017, during a college semester abroad, my daughter Leah studied in Berlin. She had three-day weekends and flights in Europe were cheap, so she got to see virtually the whole continent.

Her trip to Austria, she told me, was brief, with her only stop in Vienna. Sights there included the Beethoven Museum and the house of Sigmund Freud, founder of psychoanalysis. His patients famously lay back on a firm couch covered by a Persian carpet, staring upward while Freud would sit behind them, encouraging them to verbalize whatever came to mind (free association). He'd especially have them recount and interpret their dreams as a way of better understanding themselves. A lot of their problems got attributed to sex.

Therapy has changed a lot since then. Patients and their psychiatrists sit in chairs facing each other, like normal people. Dream analysis has dropped out of fashion. Still, Freud was revolutionary, not so much for his technique but for theorizing that a person's thoughts and feelings occur for a reason, not just randomly. Shakespeare may have implied it 300 years earlier, "Though this be madness, yet there is method in 't," but it was Freud who pioneered the science of psychology.

I asked Leah whether she had seen Freud's couch. She said no. When he fled the Nazis for London in 1938, at age eighty-two, he had shipped it with him. You can see it in London at the Freud Museum, which offers several hours' worth of displays and information and encourages visitors to "engage in a little retail therapy in the Gift Shop."

See: "What to See at the Freud Museum," *Freud Museum London*, https://www.freud.org.uk/visit/what-to-see-at-the-freud-museum/ (accessed September 2, 2023).

128. Medical Trials and Studies

The best proof of whether a treatment works or not is the randomized controlled trial, commonly called "a double-blind study." For example, if a new drug is being tested in a study, half of the participants receive the real medication and the other half get a placebo pill that looks and tastes identical but is inert, devoid of any medicine. Outside statisticians arrange the random selection and perform all analyses of drug efficacy, but never meet either patients or doctors. Neither the participants nor the clinicians know what each participant gets, thus eliminating any psychological benefit that the mere act of taking a pill might bring (a phenomenon known as the "placebo effect"). That's why this kind of study is said to be "double-blind."

One time I was reading articles in ophthalmology medical journals and was surprised to notice that they all used the term "double-masked" instead. It sure made sense. Imagine an ophthalmologist asking a patient with eye disease if they'd like to join a "double-blind" study. There'd be very few takers. When I recount this discovery to medical colleagues, they never fail to laugh.

There's also the concept of the "nocebo," the opposite of placebo ("placebo" comes from the Latin *placere* meaning "to please," "nocebo" from *nocere* "to harm"). The best examples of the nocebo effect are double-blind (or double-masked) studies in which every participant gets an empty pill without knowing it, but half receive a list of supposed side effects. Without fail, the people who receive the list experience many more phantom side effects than the group who hadn't been told about them.

The human mind is certainly fascinating.

129. Caution With the MR(Eye)

Magnetic resonance imaging (MRI) utilizes a huge magnet. As such, it's forbidden for anything containing iron to be in the vicinity of the machines; early technicians discovered this after patients' oxygen tanks started flying. It's probably no surprise then that the exam cannot be done on people with metal in their bodies, such as some pacemakers, certain old surgical clips, certain piercings, bullets, shrapnel, etc. And metal fragments in the eye.

Who'd have that? Somebody who had worked in a metal shop or any other setting where steel was sawed or hammered. Wood doesn't travel at high enough velocity to penetrate the eyeball, but metal can. A large metal shard would destroy the organ, but a tiny speck could enter the eyeball and then be sealed over. The person would have no symptoms at all, but under a big magnet like the MRI, the piece would be swept back and forth inside the eye. Ouch! (or rather, yuck!).

And in fact, there have been ongoing case reports of severe eye damage in patients with no history of previous eye injury but who had spent time in environments with risks for penetrating metal. The first report I found was from 1985, the latest from 2018. Yet the American College of Radiology's 2020 guidelines still employ old screening tools from 2013, advising precautions only for people with a known history of eye trauma, not simply having been a metalworker (protocols employ initial plain x-rays or CT scans of the eyes to detect any metal). Many institutions do go further, inquiring about past metalwork, but wouldn't it be nice if the main professional organization took the lead?

See: William M. Kelly, Patrick G. Paglen, Jack A. Pearson, Armando G. San Diego, and Murray A. Soloman, "Ferromagnetism of Intraocular Foreign Body Causes Unilateral Blindness After MR Study," *American Journal of Neuroradiology*, 7, no. 2, 243-5 (1986), https://www.ncbi.nlm.nih.gov/pmc/articles/PMC8332697/pdf/3082156.pdf (accessed December 26, 2022).

Nikolaos Mamas, Konstantinos Andreanos, Dimitrios Brouzas et al., "Acute Ocular Pain During Magnetic Resonance Imaging Due to Retained Intraocular Metallic Foreign Body: The Role of Ultrasonography and Ultrasound Biomicroscopy in Diagnosis and Management of This Condition," *Journal of Ultrasound*, 21, no. 2, 159-163 (2018), https://www.ncbi.nlm.nih.gov/pmc/articles/PMC5972104/ (accessed December 26, 2022).

ACR Committee on MR Safety, "ACR Manual of MR Safety, Version 1.0," *American College of Radiology*, 2020, https://www.acr.org/-/media/ACR/Files/Radiology-Safety/MR-Safety/Manual-on-MR-Safety.pdf (accessed December 31, 2022).

130. Useful Warnings to Prevent Epidemics

A ladies' restroom at the Moscone Convention
Center, San Francisco (courtesy of Leah Leiner, whose
father, the author, doesn't troll such venues).

131. Beware of (Some) Screening Tests

In the early 2000s, South Korea began an ambitious program to screen its citizens for various cancers. Just using simple ultrasounds, they wound up discovering an enormous number of cases of papillary thyroid cancer. Alarmed, countless patients had surgery to remove their thyroid glands. This required that they take thyroid medication the rest of their lives, and some had significant complications from the operations.

But despite all the diagnoses, the death rate from thyroid cancer didn't change at all. This meant that the surgeries didn't save lives. We've known a long time that the papillary type of thyroid cancer is extremely common. It may sit around without doing anything for a lifetime; people who have it die of something else. The dangerous medullary type of thyroid cancer is much rarer, thus was hardly detected by the ultrasounds.

When a journal article describing the uselessness of all the surgeries was published in 2014, it made big news. Patients realized this was not what they wanted and declined or refused ultrasounds and operations. South Korean thyroid specialists and surgeons decried the bad press, scolding that screening and treatment are "basic human rights." They neglected to add how they're also good income generators.

See: Hyeong Sik Ahn and H. Gilbert Welch, "South Korea's Thyroid-Cancer 'Epidemic' — Turning the Tide," *New England Journal of Medicine*, 373, no. 24, 2389-90 (2015), https://www.nejm.org/doi/10.1056/NEJMc1507622 (accessed December 26, 2022).

132. "I Want an MRI"

Patients with one pain or another often insist on an MRI. When I attempt to explain that it's not necessary, they often get upset that I'm denying them a health insurance right, and our clinical visit is, overall, far from satisfying. In general, injuries rarely require an MRI unless you're contemplating surgery, and even then, its results can be misleading. Consider my own story.

When I was fifty-nine, I tore my right anterior cruciate ligament (ACL) while scoring a soccer goal; I made a deft shot on the run around left wing. Glory was diminished by it being a parents versus young kids' game. I hobbled into my ER, the diagnosis was clinically obvious (the doc could wiggle my knee front to back, which can't happen if the ACL is intact; medically, it's a "positive Lachman test"). He ordered an MRI and sent me to orthopedics.

The first orthopedist was a youngish, strapping athletic type who said data didn't really show surgery helped people over fifty. Besides, he did autograft repairs, using one of the patient's own superfluous tendons to fix it. It was one of the most successful methods for repairing tears, but requires intensive physical therapy … and, to be honest, I looked sort of plumpish. But, he said, he'd gladly refer me to a colleague who did the easier allograft procedure, which uses cadaver ligaments. The colleague was older, with a body habitus just like mine, and eager to proceed. He noted my main health risk was the partly torn meniscus (knee cartilage), which could lead to arthritis.

I was okay with both repairs, and I had my surgery. Well, wouldn't you know it, but the first thing the doctor told me when I woke up was that my meniscus was perfectly intact. So much for the MRI. One study found that 97% of MRI's performed on adults without any knee pain or injury showed a variety of abnormalities, in other words, lots of false positives.

Low back pain is another good example of the MRI's limitations. This kind of pain is usually caused by muscle strains or ligament sprains; these can't be seen by MRI. The main findings we look for (aside from rare conditions) are bulging, herniated disks, which cause sciatica. But in studies of healthy people without any back pain, a large majority of their MRIs show "bulging herniated disks" (maybe even 100% of people over age sixty). Similar findings were found for the cervical spine among people without any neck pain. In other words, if we see a bad disk, it doesn't mean *in any way at all* that it's the cause of pain.

Orthopedists and neurosurgeons only operate if clinical symptoms match the MRI abnormality, so if the disk bulge is at the L2–L3 level, but symptoms are a classic L4–L5, no way would they proceed ("L2" = second lumbar vertebra, etc.). I once had a patient with an L4-L5 herniated disk pressing on the nerve, and classic matching symptoms—but the MRI finding was on the right, and his symptoms ran down the left leg. No surgery for him.

But there's more. Most sciatica from herniated disks gets better on its own in three to four months. Attempting surgery before that could wind up making things worse for the patient. And if surgery isn't on the horizon, there's no need for an MRI. An MRI of the spine may cost almost $1,000, so it's not something any clinician should order just for the sake of doing it, especially if its information won't change medical care.

P.S. That $1,000 figure has some caveats. In Europe it may be ten times less. Prices aren't fixed in stone (or gold). They're high here in the US because of our absurd healthcare system.

See: Laura M Horga, Anna C Hirschmann, Johann Henckel, et al., "Prevalence of Abnormal Findings in 230 Knees of Asymptomatic Adults Using 3.0 T MRI," *Skeletal Radiology*, 49, no. 7, 1099-1107 (2020), https://pubmed.ncbi.nlm.nih.gov/32060622/ (accessed March 27, 2023).

Nathan M.Wnuk, Tarik K.Alkasab, and Daniel I.Rosenthal, "Magnetic Resonance Imaging of the Lumbar Spine: Determining Clinical Impact and Potential Harm from Overuse," *The Spine Journal*, 18, no. 9, 1653-1658 (2018), https://www.sciencedirect.com/science/article/abs/pii/S1529943018301591 (accessed December 26, 2022).

Rajeev K Patel, "Lumbar Degenerative Disk Disease Workup," *Medscape*, updated September 7, 2022, https://emedicine.medscape.com/article/309767-workup#c4 (accessed December 26, 2022).

Hiroaki Nakashima, Yasutsugu Yukawa, Kota Suda, et al., "Abnormal Findings on Magnetic Resonance Images of the Cervical Spines in 1211 Asymptomatic Subjects," *Spine* (Phila Pa 1976), 40, no. 6, 392-98 (2015), https://pubmed.ncbi.nlm.nih.gov/25584950/ (accessed March 27, 2023).

133. Can You, Too, Be a Pharmacist?

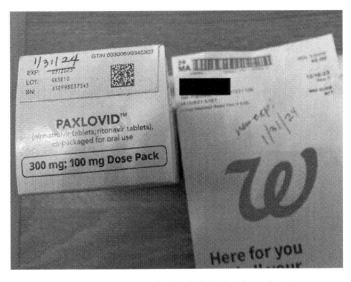

An easy way to extend the shelf life of medications.

134. Pertussis "Outbreaks"

P ertussis, aka "whooping cough," is a very contagious illness causing mild or no symptoms in adults and older children, but it can be fatal to babies. It's especially dangerous for infants under six months old, which is when the vaccination series (if received) is completed. From 2004 to 2006, several states experienced pertussis outbreaks among hospital staff, some on pediatric wards. Countless health workers were screened and given preventive antibiotics. Hundreds tested positive by polymerase chain reaction (PCR), the standard technology these days.

These cases occurred among hospital staff, but there weren't many cases reported in surrounding communities, so the Centers for Disease Control and Prevention (CDC) investigated. As it turned out, the tests were so good at detecting parts of germs that over 99 percent of tests wound up with a false-positive! Good news for the people testing "positive'" but not so good for the employers. At Dartmouth Hospital in New Hampshire, a thousand employees with mild symptoms were furloughed and another thousand were given preventive antibiotics just in case, all unnecessarily. (Whoops!)

Sometimes these germ parts found by PCR are shared by other germs that don't cause disease. Sometimes PCR detects dead germs. PCR has revolutionized laboratory medicine. But like any good thing, it needs be evaluated with at least some caution.

See: Laura Stephenson Carter, "A Rough, Tough Cough: Was It, or Wasn't It, the Whooping Kind?" *Dartmouth Medicine.* Spring 2007, https://dartmed.dartmouth.edu/spring07/html/vs_cough.php (accessed December 26, 2022). [easier to read].

Centers for Disease Control and Prevention (CDC), "Outbreaks of Respiratory Illness Mistakenly Attributed to Pertussis --- New Hampshire, Massachusetts, and Tennessee, 2004--2006," *Morbidity and Mortality Weekly Reports* (MMWR), 56, no. 33, 837-842 (2007), https://www.cdc.gov/mmwr/preview/mmwrhtml/mm5633a1.htm (accessed December 26, 2022). [very complete, very medical]

135. My Doctor Didn't Remember Me!

I'm a nurse practitioner, a primary care provider like my colleague physicians. Every so often, I see a patient whose last visit may have been several years before because they were generally healthy and not in need of regular appointments. Such a patient might enthusiastically ask, "Do you remember the back pain I had three years ago?" When I reply, "No," they're crestfallen.

I explain how it has been a long time since I last saw them. But, I add, there are some patients whom I remember very well—people with complex medical problems who come to my clinic monthly or more often. My generally healthy patient will quickly get the idea and happily respond, "Please, don't remember me."

Almost ten years ago, I had two unrelated patients, Antonia and Marcos, whom I was trying to locate in our electronic medical records system. They hadn't come to see me for a while, harbored serious illnesses, and I wanted to call them but surprisingly couldn't find their names. Fortunately, I remembered their birthdates: September 19, 1945, and June 17, 1957. How did I do that? Because they had such complicated medical histories, I was constantly looking at their charts and writing referrals by hand for years before our clinic went electronic. The birthdates did the trick. I found their medical record numbers and jotted them down for safekeeping.

But why couldn't I find them using their names? Our IT department figured out the errors: both had recently updated their registrations. In Antonia's case, an "o" in her surname had been mistyped as a zero. Marcos took more sleuthing, but a clever tech realized that the spacebar had been inadvertently tapped before the first letter in his.

I recently checked our database, and even though I haven't seen these patients since they moved away over seven years ago, I was right about the dates. You *never* want your medical provider to be able to remember your birthday by heart.

Humor: LOL

"There is nothing in the world so irresistibly contagious as laughter and good humor."

—Charles Dickens, *A Christmas Carol*

"I know not all that may be coming, but be it what it will, I'll go to it laughing."

—Herman Melville, *Moby-Dick*

"With mirth and laughter let old wrinkles come."

—William Shakespeare, *The Merchant of Venice*

136. Nary a Word

My great aunt Jenny, whom I barely ever knew, apparently had a wonderful sense of humor. According to a story I was told, she once attended a funeral where her husband, Nat, was a pallbearer. As he trudged solemnly toward the grave, striving to remain in step with the others so entrusted, Jenny in the crowd caught his eye. Silently, she looked down and pointed toward her pubis—implying that his fly was open.

It wasn't! But this was the 1930s, when caskets were hoisted up on shoulders, so Nat couldn't see. And he certainly couldn't have done anything about it. He had to walk the entire length of the procession imagining the worst.

In my mind a practical joke at a funeral, deftly performed by a simple rapid gesture without a word, is the epitome of humor.

137. Comebacks

Here are a few of the best retorts I recall hearing or reading about in recent years. I tried searching Google for other contemporary ones, but these were better (I'd never beat the classics like Oscar Wilde, Mark Twain, Churchill, etc.).

a) A woman's car broke down at a stop sign. As she tried to restart it, the car behind hers kept honking. The woman calmly got out, walked over, and politely asked the man at the wheel, "Sir, if you could help me start my car, I'd be happy to sit here and honk your horn for you."

b) Very tall people invariably get asked by strangers if they play basketball. One such man would reply, "No. Do you play miniature golf?"

c) A not-so-popular worker entered his office one morning, complaining, "I was just crossing the street now, and this idiot came zooming around the corner—he almost killed me!" Another employee opined, "That's too bad."

138. Gallows Humor

AIDS ravaged the gay community for several years before it was identified in 1981, and until effective treatment for HIV became available in 1996 and then widely prescribed (in rich countries, at least). In those early days, virtually all infected people died, on the average ten years after contracting the virus or a year after becoming ill with AIDS-related diseases. It wasn't uncommon for a thirty-year-old to have attended over fifty funerals. Sadly, there was widespread indifference throughout the United States back then, since the epidemic mostly affected specific populations marginalized by society: homosexual men, heroin users (those who inject drugs), Haitians, and people with hemophilia who had received many blood transfusions. The mainstream press as well as those living with HIV and AIDS referred to these groups as "the four H's."

Humor can help people cope. Sometimes, the more morbid it is, the better it works. A common joke told among gay men during that time was, "The hardest thing about explaining my diagnosis to my family was having to come out as Haitian."

139. Torture

My daughter and I visited the medieval walled city of Carcassonne, a UNESCO World Heritage Site in southern France. It's beautifully preserved; the main incongruity are the countless tourist shops occupying every house. Among the buildings was a torture museum, where you could see every imaginable gruesome way people had devised to inflict pain on others. It was the first time I saw a real guillotine; it seemed small and mundane, not fearsome at all. The only brutal instrument I've subconsciously chosen to recall was a vice for "bad musicians," which crushed their fingers.

I had studied basic French in high school and learned to speak it well in the early 1970s when I worked several seasons in Swiss vineyards. But by 2017, the language had all but disappeared from my brain. At the museum's entry, a bored and weary woman was sitting on a stool in blazing hot sun, collecting tickets. I took a chance, venturing to say in French, "Is sitting here torture?" She readily agreed and laughed. I felt proud of my renewed fluency.

The museum exit led through a small café, which was empty at the time, save for a waiter. So I asked him, again in French, "Do people dare eat in a torture museum's bistro?" Offended, he replied indignantly, "We have a very nice restaurant here." At least I can still communicate somewhat, I thought to myself as I hurried off.

140. On Laughter

As part of my personal philosophy, I consider it a virtue to join with others in laughter. If I can say something daily that makes someone smile, I'm happy with myself. This effort might be as minimal as passing a stranger in Golden Gate Park and, in response to their nicety like "Beautiful day," offering the quip, "Global warming has its benefits." My remarks are invariably spontaneous.

My best—again in the park—occurred when I was going down some steps as a group was heading up. One man, likely in his late twenties and lugging a baby stroller for his friends, admonished the others, "Watch out. Carrying a child is a serious business." I interjected, "But you didn't do it for nine months!" His friends burst out in laughter. One woman acknowledged me with a "Thank you." I smiled back and scurried on.

Sometimes my quips are not so well-received. In a diner while in college, I pointed out a "minute steak" ("my-NOOT") on the menu. And once, after dark, some friends and I passed a group of people distressed to discover they'd accidentally left their headlights on. I reassured them, "Your lights are on—that means the battery still works. Imagine if you'd come back to your car and the lights were off!" They were unappreciative.

Laughter has a variety of health benefits. It can ameliorate pain, as literary editor and author Norman Cousins discovered, enduring crippling arthritis outbreaks when watching old Marx Brothers comedies. Laughter reduces stress hormones, increases neurotransmitters which relieve depression, and releases endorphins (our natural opioids) a little like sex does. Anthropologists note how laughter is found in all societies, including apes, and even among rats. It may confer survival benefits, enhance social connections, and attract sexual partners.

If this book has inspired you to laugh, I feel proud to have achieved my goal (even if you read it without buying it).

See: Giovanni Sabato, "What's So Funny? The Science of Why We Laugh," *Scientific American*, June 26, 2019, https://www.scientificamerican.com/article/whats-so-funny-the-science-of-why-we-laugh/ (accessed January 23, 2023).

JongEun Yim, "Therapeutic Benefits of Laughter in Mental Health: A Theoretical Review," *Tohoku Journal of Experimental Medicine*, 239, No. 3, 243-249 (2016), https://pubmed.ncbi.nlm.nih.gov/27439375/ (accessed February 6, 2023).

Don Colburn, "Norman Cousins, Still Laughing," *Washington Post*, October 21, 1986, https://www.washingtonpost.com/archive/lifestyle/wellness/1986/10/21/norman-cousins-still-laughing/e17f23cb-3e8c-4f58-b907-2dcd00326e22/ (accessed February 13, 2023).

Acknowledgments

This section probably shouldn't be funny. Profuse thank you's to all who've inspired and encouraged me, inadvertently or not: my deceased parents George & Malvina, who surely contributed to my overall joie de vivre; my wife Mary and our daughters Rebecca and Leah, for the countless occasions they refused to laugh at my wit; my formative college years at the University of Chicago, and the sarcastic songs of Tom Lehrer; friends and relatives renamed, who contributed their share of stories and anecdotes; my many more friends and relatives present and past throughout the country and world, who keep me upbeat without their having the least idea; colleagues at work, who tolerate my frequent quips while they're trying to concentrate; my sister Alice, my niece Caroline and nephew-in-law Brian, for their suggestions and encouragement upon graciously reading my drafts; copyeditors Adam Rosen and Erin Brenner who read different sections, for their many valuable suggestions (I take full responsibility for the few I declined); proofreaders Gabriela Tully Claymore and Rebecca Leiner, for meticulously proofreading different parts; illustrator L. Plume, both stellar and witty; designer Victoria Wolf, for her skill and insight; and surely many others whom I apologetically fail to recall. Again, thank you all so much (sincerely repetitious, since a paragraph should have at least three sentences).

About the Illustrator

L. Plume is a digital artist from the Pacific Northwest. She can be contacted through email at: l.plume.art@gmail.com.

About the Author

Go back to the beginning (Introduction).